WHAT PEOPLE

TEN LIES

Christ nailed Satan with His observation that he is a liar and a mur— 8:44). Martin Luther often called attention to the devil's modus operandi: he appears as a black devil to lure us into the pursuit of outright sin, but even more formidably he attacks us by appearing as a white devil, a seeming paragon of godly piety. Jones confronts ten of the white devil's lies that strike at the heart of our humanity, our relationship with God. Satan tries to kill us by separating us from God either through pride in our works or despair of God's forgiveness and liberation from sin. Jones's pastoral experience and skill emerge in his cultivation of the reader's competence in confronting and dismissing the fears and falsities that Satan cultivates through his lies. This book thus opens the way to peace and joy in the liberated life we have through Christ's death and resurrection.

Rev. Dr. Robert Kolb, professor emeritus of systematic theology, Concordia Seminary, St. Louis

In *Ten Lies Satan Loves to Tell*, Andrew bravely leans into the uncomfortable darkness and shines a light of truth. With wisdom and clarity, Andrew's words guide us to see the heart of God and the endless beauty of His grace. Page after page, Andrew boldly calls out the evil work of Satan, reminding us of God's kind love and encouraging us to remain steadfast in the hope of Christ until He comes again. This is an excellent book for anyone who follows Jesus.

Tanner Olson, author and poet, writtentospeak.com

As a gracious teacher and pastor, Andrew's heart shines through in this book, guiding us to a deeper understanding of God's rich truths. He shows us how living in fear means falling prey to Satan's favorite deceptions. Page after page, Andrew shows us the truth found in Scripture—our ultimate hope against the crippling fear Satan would have us embrace. This book powerfully reminds us that God's perfect love, shown in Scripture and through His Son, Jesus, can be our life's foundation.

Michelle Diercks, author, speaker, and podcast host

I really enjoyed this quick but deep read. Andy does a great job of breaking down ten lies and struggles that we all encounter. He not only gives us ways to combat these lies and live a godly life but also reminds us that we do not suffer alone, pointing us back to Scripture. All of this is rooted in the beginning, in the Garden of Eden, where Satan told the first and biggest lie that impacts us still today. Readers will connect instantly and be able to tackle the lies of Satan and this world with the truth: the Gospel.

Rehema Kavugha, Synod relations director, Lutheran Church
Extension Fund

Sometimes what you read is precisely the thing you need. In an age when many cannot tell the difference between lies and truth—or the mouths from which those two things emanate—this book is one we all need. With clarity and concision, demonstrating biblical depth and breadth, Andrew Jones exposes the core of Satan's lies and shifts the focus from who you are to whose you are. In doing so, he helps us hear the voice of the One whose native tongue is not lies but truth, not death but life itself.

Rev. Dr. Matthew Borrasso, pastor, Trinity Lutheran Church,
Lexington Park, Maryland; adjunct faculty, Concordia University,
St. Paul, and Concordia University Texas

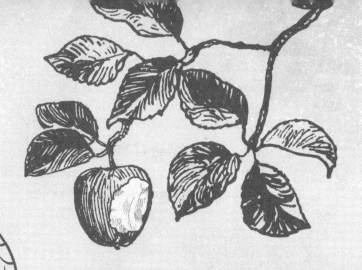

TEN LIES SATAN LOVES TO TELL

ANDREW R. JONES

CONCORDIA PUBLISHING HOUSE • SAINT LOUIS

For my grandparents—Herman and Helen,
Milton and Marian—who each taught me the
undeniable power of telling the truth

Published by Concordia Publishing House
3558 S. Jefferson Ave., St. Louis, MO 63118-3968
1-800-325-3040 • cph.org

Manufactured in the United States of America

2 3 4 5 6 7 8 9 10   33 32 31 30 29 28 27 26 25

CONTENTS

INTRODUCTION

SATAN—THE FATHER OF LIES

Satan is real. Satan is dangerous. He is dedicated to dismantling God's kingdom and God's people. One of Satan's primary tactics is deception. In John 8, Jesus exposes Satan as "a liar and the father of lies" (v. 44). Every time Satan appears in the Scriptures, he is lying, deceiving, and seeking the destruction of God's people. Satan's ultimate goal is to lead God's people as far away from God as possible. Satan assaults us by leading us ever toward present and eternal suffering.

Lies are the inception of all suffering. Lies are at the center of humanity's fall into sin. Lies lead to death. Satan is ever at work against God, and oftentimes Satan uses his allies—sin and death—as tools in the war against God's people.

Each sin that you or I participate in is rooted in a lie we have believed about ourselves or about God. In this book, we will seek to expose some of Satan's favorite lies that assault us.

As we get started, I want to set some expectations for what this book is about and what it is not about. This book seeks to expose Satan's lies, to help people recognize those lies, and to lead people away from the influence of Satan's lies. This book seeks to lead people ever toward the truth of Jesus, His kingdom, and the promised eternal life that awaits God's people.

This book is not seeking to convince you that Satan is real. The words of Jesus tell us that Satan is real and fighting against us in a cosmic spiritual battle. I trust that Jesus is telling us the truth, and I write from that perspective.

> *This book seeks to lead people ever toward the truth of Jesus.*

To that end, this is not an apologetics book. It is not meant to be used as a defense of the Christian faith against those who do not believe. This book is a handbook for those who believe in Jesus. It is a resource meant to be used by God's people against Satan and Satan's lies.

Moreover, this is not a book of shame but one of encouragement. It is a book of realization, not one of pointing fingers and pointing out failures. It is a handbook for each reader (whether read alone or in community) to help extract God's people from the lies Satan tells them.

The ten lies this book highlights are lies Satan uses in the Scriptures and continues to tell even now. These are lies Satan has told me, lies Satan has told my family and friends, parishioners and students. This is a book about the lies Satan loves to tell you, dear reader. Yet, as I said, this book is not intended to shame you. It is intended to liberate you from Satan's lies with the truth of Jesus. I would encourage you to read this book with an eye toward how Satan is lying to *you*, not how Satan might be lying to others. Think of this as looking at the log in one's own eye, not a matter of the speck in someone else's eye (see Matthew 7:1–5).

Jesus is our only hope and protection against Satan.

Ultimately, this book is my attempt to share with you all the contours of the logs I have been struggling to extract from my own eyes.

Furthermore, this is not a book about American (or any other) culture wars. It is not as if Satan has chosen to lie to some people and not to others. Satan lies to everyone. Our political preferences, denominational affiliations, and cultural heritages are not exemptions or protections against Satan. Jesus is our only hope and protection against Satan. While I will look at how Satan repeats his lies in our world today, political hot-button issues will not be talked about, even ones you may rightly care deeply about.

I do not address such topics on purpose, because the inclusion of such topics has two potential outcomes I wish to avoid. First, if I speak about a political issue pointing out the lies of your political opponents, Satan will tempt you to think you are exempt from that lie, when you are not. No one is exempt from Satan's lies. He speaks them to everyone, even to Jesus. Second, if I speak about a political issue and point out lies your political opponents are struggling with, it is unlikely that such commentary from me will assist you in loving your politically opposed neighbor. Calling out the lies of opponents often increases our own self-righteousness and encourages us toward division and hatred. Hate and division are also tactics of Satan.

This is a book about lies Satan has repeated for thousands of years, spanning numerous cultures and languages. As Jesus says of Satan, "When he lies, he speaks out of his own character" (John 8:44). Or as the NIV puts it, "When he lies, he speaks his native language."

Satan has told innumerable lies to God's people. The reason I have chosen to highlight these ten lies is that I see their origins from Satan's own words and actions in the Scriptures. I see them repeated in the Scriptures, causing devastation to God's people. And I see them repeated in our world today and in my own life. These lies attack God's people as they seek to follow Him in faith.

THE CYCLICAL LIFE OF FAITH

The longest chapter in the Bible is Psalm 119. Martin Luther held up Psalm 119 as a masterful example of the Christian life. Within the psalm, Luther saw a cyclical reality that trained God's people for a life of faith. He labeled this journey with the Latin phrase *oratio, meditatio, tentatio*. That is, *prayer, meditation*, and *temptation*. As we enter God's Word, we pray for the Holy Spirit to guide us into all truth. We meditate on God's Word by asking questions and listening with curiosity to what God reveals through His Word.

But after we have prayed and meditated on God's Word, something happens that seems counterintuitive and counterproductive to our learning from the Lord and our life of faith: we are attacked by Satan. Luther writes, "For as soon as God's Word takes root and grows in you, the devil will harry you, and will make a real doctor of you, and by his assaults will teach you to seek and love God's Word."

Satan seeks to drive us away from God and His Word with these attacks. But God uses Satan's attacks to drive us back to Himself—to prayer and to Scripture.

Again, Luther insightfully shows us this, saying, "This is the touchstone which teaches you not only to know and understand, but also to experience how right, how true, how sweet, how lovely, how mighty, how comforting God's Word is, wisdom beyond all wisdom."[1]

> *God uses Satan's attacks to drive us back to Himself— to prayer and to Scripture.*

In this way, we see a pattern in the life of faith that Joseph articulates toward the end of Genesis. After Joseph was sold into slavery by his brothers, God raised Joseph up to save Egypt and many neighboring nations from famine. After the death of their father, Jacob, Joseph's brothers still feared that Joseph would destroy them, so they begged for his mercy. But Joseph said this to his brothers: "As for you, you meant evil against me, but God meant it for good" (Genesis 50:20).[2]

Satan attacks and means evil against us, but God always intends for such attacks to drive us back into conversation with Him in prayer and into further meditation on the sweet comfort of His Word.

This cycle of prayer, meditation, and the assaults of Satan is a marked pattern in the life of every Christian. It is our cross to pick up daily and bear in faith until the return of Jesus.

While my first book, *Ten Questions to Ask Every Time You Read the Bible,* was about *meditatio,* meditation on the Scriptures, this book is a book of *tentatio,* temptation, the assaults of the devil. I believe the main weapon in Satan's arsenal of assault is lies.

Satan lies to increase our suffering. Satan uses our suffering as a means to turn us away from God. God uses our suffering to turn us

---

1   The two Luther quotations are from *Luther's Works,* volume 34, pp. 286–87.
2   For further study on Joseph and this particular scene, I recommend Donna Snow's *Meant for Good: A Study of Joseph* (St. Louis: Concordia Publishing House, 2023).

toward Himself, to turn us toward prayer and praise, to turn us toward meditation on His Word of grace and truth.

SATAN'S CHAOTIC DESIRED OUTCOME

Satan wants us to abandon God's Word and to break every instruction and commandment God has given us. Many of Satan's lies are directly in contrast to God's Word of the Ten Commandments. The Second Commandment (by Lutheran counting) says, "You shall not misuse the name of the LORD your God."[3] This seems a favorite of Satan's to break. Consider how Satan uses God's name in Genesis 3: "Did God actually say . . . ?" (v. 1). "You will not surely die. For God knows . . ." (vv. 4–5). Or in Matthew 4: "If You are the Son of God, . . ." (vv. 3, 6). Satan constantly misuses God's name by casting aspersions on what God says. Satan wants us to test God, to prove God wrong, to seize for ourselves a level of power and control that belongs rightly to God.

Luther asks of the Second Commandment, "What does this mean?" Luther's answer is "We should fear and love God so that we do not curse, swear, use satanic arts, lie, or deceive by His name, but call upon it in every trouble, pray, praise, and give thanks."[4] In German (the language Luther was writing in), the phrase translated as "use satanic arts" is more closely related to magic, conjuring, or witchcraft. Yet I like the phrase "satanic arts" here, especially since it is followed by "lie, or deceive," because of all the arts Satan uses, lying and deception are the most common and perhaps the least obvious.

As Commandments Two through Ten are each a variation on breaking the First, so all of Satan's lies draw us back to the first lie—you cannot trust God—and the First Commandment, "You shall have no other gods."

---

3 Small Catechism.
4 Small Catechism, explanation of the Second Commandment.

In this way, we also see that the ten lies in this book feed into one another. If we cannot trust God (Lie 1), then God must not love us (Lie 7). If we deserve more (Lie 3), then we need to seize more control to get it (Lie 4). If we must save ourselves (Lie 8), then we need to cover up our sins (Lie 6). If we cover up our sins, our performance will be judged more favorably (Lie 2). And so on.

Satan does not operate in such a way that makes it easy to fight his lies and overcome them. Indeed, this book seems out of order no matter what order I choose. Satan is organized when it suits him and chaotic when it suits him. Satan isolates when it suits him and lies to entire communities when it suits him. Satan is silent when it suits him. Satan whispers when it suits him. And Satan shouts when it suits him. We should never assume that we fully understand Satan's tactics. This book is not comprehensive, nor can any book on the subject be so.

Of all the arts Satan uses, lying and deception are the most common.

In Ephesians 6, Paul writes about the armor of God. One piece we hear about is the shield of faith: "In all circumstances take up the shield of faith, with which you can extinguish all the flaming darts of the evil one" (v. 16). Shields in Paul's time were covered in leather that had been soaked so that if a flaming arrow hit the shield, the fire would be immediately extinguished.

Satan's lies are fiery darts, aimed with both deadly accuracy and scattershot chaos. Our faith in Jesus acts as a shield against these fiery darts. I would be honored if you considered this book a patch of soaked leather for your shield of faith.

BUT . . . HASN'T JESUS DEFEATED SATAN? WHY DO WE NEED THIS BOOK?

One of the most common questions I hear on this topic is related to a confusion about whether Satan is still dangerous to us. The apostle Peter writes, "Your adversary the devil prowls around like a roaring lion, seeking someone to devour" (1 Peter 5:8). Peter wrote those words a few decades after Jesus suffered, died, rose from the dead, ascended into heaven, and was enthroned with all power and authority. Hence, we may ask ourselves, "Didn't Jesus defeat Satan? Why is Satan still a problem today?" Yes, indeed, Jesus defeated Satan. Satan is a conquered enemy, just as sin and death are conquered enemies. Jesus forgives our sin by His death on the cross, but we still sin. Jesus triumphed over death by His resurrection, but we still die. We await a promised eternal life in the new creation that is free from sin, death, and the devil, but all three conquered enemies still harass us until Jesus returns.

For me, the best illustration of Satan's actions today comes from *The Lord of the Rings: The Return of the King*. While the films leave this out, author J. R. R. Tolkien has a chapter toward the end of the series called "The Scouring of the Shire." The wizard Saruman is a traitor. He betrays all his former allies and joins with the dark lord Sauron, only to be defeated by his former allies. His powers are stripped. His wizard's staff is broken. Yet he remains dangerous. He still has his voice. And Saruman's voice speaks deception and cruelty. Saruman makes his way to the Shire, the home of the hobbits, and enslaves them through nothing but lies and threats alone.

Scripture does not reveal how Satan's power on earth is qualitatively different before and after the death and resurrection of Jesus. But Satan is defeated to be sure. He prowls around, roaring, lying, threatening. As one of my parishioners pointed out to me, lions who prowl do not tend to roar. Prowling is an act of secrecy. Roaring is an act that reveals and terrifies. Satan prowls and roars in dissonant chaos. He still seeks to destroy us, devour us, and drag us into the abyss with him, further down and further away from the Lord. Indeed, that is the devil's fate. But Satan does so now only in prideful refusal to see the truth. Satan will not defeat God. Satan will not rule over the heavens and the earth. Satan lost the decisive battle on Easter Sunday, when Jesus rose from the dead, just as Saruman lost when his staff was broken and his powers were stripped. But both Satan and Saruman continue on in their stories with their lies and threats and are still dangerous and capable of producing much suffering.

SATAN IN THE SCRIPTURES

There are a few places in the Old Testament where Satan is mentioned, but every author of the New Testament mentions Satan at some point in his writings. All told, Satan appears fewer times than you might think on the pages of the Scriptures. While his influence is prevalent throughout, he is not always named as the source of the calamity that is occurring. The places Satan speaks, however, paint a picture of his character and tactics that will serve as the basis for the ten lies we will discuss in this book.

> *Satan lost the decisive battle on Easter Sunday, when Jesus rose from the dead.*

Each lie's inception occurs in Genesis 3, in the Garden of Eden, as Satan tempts Adam and Eve into sin and brings about the fall of all creation. Satan's temptation of Jesus in the wilderness, as recorded in Matthew 4:1–11 and Luke 4:1–13, will be revisited several times throughout the following chapters, as will Satan's role in the opening chapters of the book of Job.

CONTOURS OF EACH CHAPTER

Each chapter of this book will be dedicated to exposing one of Satan's often repeated lies. With each lie, we will dig into that lie's origins. We will unmask the outcome Satan desires from this lie (which is why he loves to tell it). We will analyze the fears Satan preys on when using that particular lie. We will trace the repetition of the lie in the Bible as well as the repetition of the lie in the world today. But each chapter will turn to basking in the truth of Jesus. We will showcase God's desired outcome for us and our salvation. We will take comfort in God's love, which quiets the fears that Satan's lies prey on. Finally, the end of each chapter has questions for reflection and Bible passages for further meditation on the truth of Jesus.

As we begin this book of Satan's lies (*tentatio*), let us pray (*oratio*) and meditate (*meditatio*) briefly on a text of the Scriptures.

> Lord Jesus, You came into our world to forgive sin, defeat death, and conquer Satan. As we embark on a journey to uncover Satan's lies, permeate our minds with Your truth so that we might live more faithfully under You in Your kingdom, for You live and reign with the Father and the Holy Spirit, one God, now and forever. Amen.

Take a minute to ponder the following Scripture passage.

> Put on then, as God's chosen ones, holy and beloved, compassionate hearts, kindness, humility, meekness, and patience, bearing with one another and, if one has a complaint against another, forgiving each other; as the Lord has forgiven you, so you also must forgive. And above all these put on love, which binds everything together in perfect harmony. (Colossians 3:12–14)

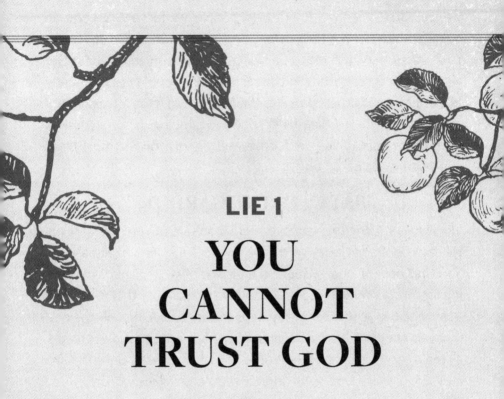

LIE 1

YOU CANNOT TRUST GOD

Trust is central to our lives and relationships. When we trust people, we feel safe. When we do not trust people, we feel anxious and on edge. Consider how it feels to be riding in a car with a safe driver you trust versus how it feels to be riding in a car with an erratic driver whom you regret getting in the car with. Being able to confidently place our trust in others provides stability in life. If we lack trustworthy relationships, life will likely be chaotic and tumultuous. Satan desires such chaos in our lives. He focuses our distrust on the most trustworthy one of all: God.

SATAN IN THE GARDEN

In Genesis 3, the first words out of Satan's mouth are a deception. He casts doubt on God's Word as he says to Eve, "Did God actually say, 'You shall not eat of any tree in the garden'?" (v. 1). This is misleading for a very simple reason: God did not actually say that. God gave Adam and Eve all the rest of the trees to eat, forbidding only the one that was not good for them. Satan knows full well God did not forbid all the trees. But Satan's intention is to cast aspersions on what God has said, to make God seem unreasonable and untrustworthy.

Eve defends God to Satan. She tells him plainly, "We may eat of the fruit of the trees in the garden" (v. 2). But there is one tree that Adam and Eve are not supposed to eat from. So Eve relays that information as well: "But God said, 'You shall not eat of the fruit of the tree that is in the midst of the garden, neither shall you touch it, lest you die'" (v. 3).

Satan seizes on Eve's defense of God and speaks another deceptive line that continues to cast doubt on God's trustworthiness. Satan begins, "You will not surely die" (v. 4). This is both true and false. Adam and Eve will die as a result of eating the fruit of this tree. They will be cast out of the Garden of Eden, be removed from their access to the tree of life, and die, returning to the dust. But they will not die right away.

In this way, Satan also seizes on the addition Eve relays to God's restriction. Eve's words "neither shall you touch it" are not recorded as part of the instruction God gave to Adam in Genesis 2:16–17. Satan has promised Eve that she will not surely die when she eats of the fruit nor when she touches the fruit. As Eve reaches out and touches the fruit from the tree and does not drop dead immediately, perhaps it makes Satan seem more trustworthy to Eve. Eve will not die as a result of touching the fruit, but she will die as a result of eating the fruit, just as God said. God remains trustworthy.

Satan continues, "For God knows that when you eat of it your eyes will be opened, and you will be like God, knowing good and evil" (Genesis 3:5). Here Satan deceives with the truth. Eve's eyes will be opened. She will be like God in that she will know good and evil.

But notice the insinuation behind this truth. Satan is telling Eve that God is holding out on her. Satan is telling Eve that God does not have her best interests in mind. Satan is calling God a liar. Satan's overarching lie in all of this is that Eve cannot trust God.

Furthermore, Satan deceives not only with questions and half-truths but also with omissions. What Satan omits is that Eve is already like God in other ways that she will lose once she eats of this fruit. Like God, Eve is sinless. Like God, Eve is holy. Like God, Eve is perfect. Eve is made in God's image, after His likeness. But after she eats of this fruit, she will

Satan's overarching lie in all of this is that Eve cannot trust God.

be sinful, cursed, blemished. She will still be God's creation, made in His image, but that image will be marred, distorted, veiled. Yes, Eve will gain the knowledge of good and evil and be like God in that one respect, but she will lose her likeness to God in so many other ways.

Eve is deceived into giving up all the ways she is like God in order to obtain one similarity she is missing, a similarity to God that she does not need, a similarity that will not move her closer to God as promised but will only exile her from the paradise of God's presence.

SATAN'S DESIRED OUTCOME

Satan wants God's people to hate God. Satan wants God's people to be distant, detached, and disinterested. What better way to get people to turn away from God than to convince them that they cannot trust Him?

Are there people in your life whom you do not trust? How much time do you choose to spend with such people? Probably as little as possible. None, if it can be managed.

If we cannot trust someone, we feel anxious in that person's presence. We feel wary, guarded, and suspicious. We may even feel like we are holding in a breath. We feel relief when we leave the person's presence, like we can finally exhale. This is the opposite of the relationship God desires with His people. God wants us to feel relief and comfort in His presence, not unease. God wants us to trust Him and His Word, not be filled with fear, doubt, and reluctance every time we hear His name and His Word.

Satan cannot keep God away from us.

Satan cannot keep God away from us. God will always keep pursuing us, calling us back to Him. Satan's only hope to destroy our relationship with God is to mess it up on our end, to keep us turning ever away from God, because God will never give up on us. Satan's aim is to warp our relationship with God into one of silence, where God's Word falls on our deaf ears and we speak no words to God at all. That is the fruit of distrust. That is the goal behind this lie: Distance. Silence. Hatred.

THE FEAR BEHIND THE LIE

Satan is the opposite of God. God's native language is truth. Satan's native language is lies. God is love. Satan is fear. First John 4:18 says, "There is no fear in love, but perfect love casts out fear."

As Satan assaults God's people, he seeks to distort these words of Scripture and bring about his own distorted version: "Fear casts out love."

Behind many of the lies Satan tells us, our own fears lurk in the background. Satan preys on those fears. Fear is not necessarily sinful. I have a healthy fear of heights, which prevents me from putting myself in dangerous situations. But even such healthy fears highlight our weaknesses. I am afraid of heights because I am afraid to die. Perhaps you are afraid of rejection or being unloved or not having purpose. Such fears can make us vulnerable, as we often overcompensate to prevent our fears from becoming reality. Satan notices our vulnerabilities and seeks to attack those weak points with precision. Fear is one of Satan's favorite allies, which is not surprising. Fear often makes us want to hide. And if we are hiding, we are isolated. If we are hiding, we have distanced ourselves from God.

Consider what Adam says to God in the Garden of Eden after he and Eve fall into sin: "I heard the sound of You in the garden, and I was afraid, because I was naked, and I hid myself" (Genesis 3:10). Fear causes Adam and Eve to hide, to flee from the presence of God. God, of course, comes looking for them. God, of course, finds them and repairs the relationships (even promising in that same chapter the ultimate repair that we know has arrived in Jesus).

I believe that the fear connected with the lie "You cannot trust God" is the fear of being wrong, the fear of being deceived.

A term that has come into common usage recently, and perfectly describes Satan's tactics, is *gaslight.* To gaslight someone is to manipulate them by making them question and doubt their own memory, judgment, and intuition. Satan is the original gaslighter. One of the tactics gaslighters use is to accuse their opposition of the very thing they themselves are guilty of.

Imagine two children playing outside, and one breaks a window. The guilty one comes forward first and falsely accuses the innocent one saying, "Well, my friend broke the window." When the innocent child arises and truthfully says, "No, I didn't break it! You broke it," it is already too late. One is the truth and the other a lie, but the truth and the lie sound remarkably alike. Indeed, the lie often sounds better.

Perhaps the guilty gaslighter speaks gently, calmly, maybe even adding that it was an accident in the accusation. But the wrongly accused truth-teller speaks with anxiety and indignation, for they have done nothing wrong and feel desperate to defend themselves. By comparison, the gaslighter seems reasonable, honorable, and sensible, while the wrongfully accused sounds petty and childish.

Satan is a liar. So how would Satan gaslight us about God? By calling God a liar. Satan deceives us by trying to convince us that God has deceived us. Satan accuses God of the very crimes Satan himself has committed.

Eve falls victim to Satan's manipulation. I would invite you to put yourself in Eve's position. Perhaps Eve is afraid of being mistaken, deceived, wrong about what she believes, what she knows, who she trusts. In her entire life, she has never encountered someone or something that did not have her best interests in mind. Satan gaslights Eve by suggesting that God does not have her best interests in mind. Before Eve realizes Satan's character, her mind

> *Satan accuses God of the very crimes Satan himself has committed.*

is opened to the possibility that God might not have her best interests in mind.

Satan pries Eve's mind open to the possibility that God might not be trustworthy. Satan preys on a fear he invented for Eve—that she might be wrong. Satan embeds the fear in her and then preys on it.

In your own life, how do you feel when you discover that you are wrong about something? How do you react? Do you get a bit defensive? Do you perhaps deflect the blame away from yourself and onto others? Do you get angry with whomever or whatever disappointed you?

Satan convinces Eve that she is wrong about God and the forbidden fruit. But after Eve takes and eats and gives some to Adam to take and eat, they realize that what they were wrong about was listening to Satan. God's Word proved true. Satan's word proved false. They were wrong to trust Satan.

When God comes looking for Adam and Eve and finds them hiding, their reactions to being wrong come out in their answers. Adam says, "The woman whom You gave to be with me, she gave me fruit of the tree, and I ate" (Genesis 3:12). In being wrong, Adam blames Eve, and Adam blames God. Eve gave him the fruit. God gave Adam this woman. Adam stands defensive, afraid of being wrong. If you have ever heard of Luther or other theologians using the phrase "the old Adam," this posture of fear and self-justification is at the heart of that phrase. Fear turns human beings in on themselves. Fear makes us seek to protect what is most important. And sadly, so often what is most important to Adam and to us is nothing but ourselves. Adam takes the two things that should be the most important to him—God and Eve—and throws both under the bus to remove any perception of his being in the wrong.

THE LIE REPEATED IN THE BIBLE

SATAN IN THE WILDERNESS

The clearest case of this lie being repeated is Jesus' temptation in the wilderness in Matthew 4:1–11 and Luke 4:1–13.[5] Matthew writes that immediately after Jesus is baptized in the Jordan River by John the Baptist, Jesus is then "led up by the Spirit into the wilderness to be tempted by the devil" (Matthew 4:1). The first word out Satan's mouth might be his favorite word: *if*. Satan begins his temptation by saying, "If You are the Son of God . . ." (v. 3). Why does Satan say this? Because God the Father had just proclaimed from heaven at Jesus' Baptism, "This is My beloved Son, with whom I am well pleased" (Matthew 3:17).

Satan's use of "If You are the Son of God . . ." is just another way of saying, "Did God actually say . . . ?"

Much like with Eve, Satan wants Jesus to distrust God's Word. Satan tries to persuade Jesus to take things into His own hands. In effect, Satan is saying to Jesus, "You cannot simply trust God's Word that You are His Son. You should test that out. Prove it. Find assurance by using Your power, by testing God's Word. Turn these stones to bread. Jump off the temple. The actual Son of God could do such things." We will talk about these lies more in depth in subsequent chapters.

THE PARABLE OF THE SOWER

Jesus begins the parable of the sower with these words: "A sower went out to sow. And as he sowed, some seeds fell along the path, and the birds came and devoured them" (Matthew 13:3–4). As Jesus explains this parable, He says, "When anyone hears the word of the kingdom and does not understand it, the evil one comes and snatches

---

5 Mark 1:12–13 also records the temptation of Jesus but does not record Satan's dialogue with Jesus.

away what has been sown in his heart. This is what was sown along the path" (v. 19).

When God's Word is proclaimed, the evil one (Satan) flies around, trying to devour the Word before it can take root. Satan snatches the Word away. He does not let understanding come to the heart where God's Word has been planted. Satan prevents God's Word from taking root in whatever way he can. Sometimes the hearts of those hearing are so hard that Satan's work is already done. Sometimes Satan distracts with more pressing matters, preventing hearts from taking the time to understand. Sometimes Satan repeats this very lie that hardens hearts again and again: "You cannot trust God. You cannot trust His Word. Let me take that seed for you so you do not have to think about it."

JEREMIAH

There are also several instances in the Scriptures where God sends His Word through one of His prophets but the prophet is not received by the people. The people do not trust God's Word.

Jeremiah has many struggles getting God's people to listen to God's Word. On one occasion, God's people are fighting against the Babylonians. As the Babylonians are about to destroy Jerusalem and exile God's people, Jeremiah delivers this Word to God's people:

> Thus says the LORD: He who stays in this city shall die by the sword, by famine, and by pestilence, but he who goes out to the Chaldeans shall live. He shall have his life as a prize of war, and live. Thus says the LORD: This city shall surely be given into the hand of the army of the king of Babylon and be taken. (Jeremiah 38:2–3)

How do the people respond? They go to their king, Zedekiah, and say,

> Let this man be put to death, for he is weakening the hands of the soldiers who are left in this city, and the hands of all the people, by speaking such words to them. For this man is not seeking the welfare of this people, but their harm. (v. 4)

The people do not believe Jeremiah's word. They do not believe God's Word. They still think they can defeat the Babylonians by their own earthly power. The king acquiesces to the people, who then trap Jeremiah in an empty cistern (see v. 6).

As the people reject Jeremiah's word, they reject God's Word. Even though Jeremiah is telling the truth, they treat him like a treasonous traitor. They leave him for dead in the mud of a cistern. This is similar to the way Jesus was treated by His own people when He stood trial before the chief priests and the scribes, left for dead on the cross through the hands of an acquiescing ruler.

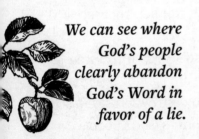

We can see where God's people clearly abandon God's Word in favor of a lie.

Satan's role in the Jeremiah story is not explicit, but we can see where God's people clearly abandon God's Word in favor of a lie. Through Jeremiah, God tells the people to give up, surrender, and live. Satan lies by repeating this chapter's lie: "You cannot trust God. You cannot trust this so-called prophet. Look, his words are making you lose the battle. Best to shut him up and keep fighting." Satan's desired effect of distance from God and disinterest in His Word is accomplished—at least for a time. Jeremiah is eventually delivered from the cistern. He repeats God's message to the king, but still nobody wants to hear the bad news Jeremiah has from the Lord. Many of God's people are needlessly destroyed because of Satan's lie, which is exactly what Satan wants. Though many people do not survive, some do. God preserves a remnant of people who are exiled from their homeland for decades, but eventually, some of them and their descendants return. You can read their stories in the biblical books of Ezra, Nehemiah, and Haggai.

When God's people reject God's prophets, they reject God's Word. When God's people reject God's Word, they are lowering their shields of faith and allowing Satan's fiery, lie-filled darts to pierce through.

THE LIE REPEATED IN OUR WORLD

There are so many places in our world where Satan seeks to cast doubt on God and His Word. The misdirection of "Did God actually say . . . ?" can be finished with nearly any statement to destabilize God's people.

Did God actually say you should love your enemies? Even *them*?

Did Jesus actually claim to be divine? Surely, there's just been a misunderstanding.

Did Jesus really perform *all* those miracles or is that a bit exaggerated?

Did Jesus *physically* rise from the dead or is this all meant to be understood more spiritually?

Did God really say (fill in the blank with your favorite sin) is not okay?

And we will see how the subsequent lies all find their muddy path back to this first sulfur pit of Satan's filth.

In each case, Satan wants us to question whether God's promises are trustworthy; he encourages us to place our trust somewhere else. Anywhere else. Inevitably, Satan wants us to place our trust in his deceptions and lies rather than in God's Word of truth.

Satan interlinks related lies in a logical progression. If we cannot trust God, then we cannot trust God's Word. If we cannot trust God's Word, then we

> *Satan wants us to place our trust in his deceptions and lies rather than in God's Word of truth.*

cannot trust His prophets and apostles. If we cannot trust His prophets and apostles, then we cannot trust the Scriptures. If we cannot trust all these things, how can we be sure our sins are forgiven? How can we be sure Jesus rose from the dead? How can we be sure Jesus was real at all?

Satan casts suspicion on every level listed above. Worse, the progression above works in the opposite direction. Satan tries to move us up and down this logical ladder of lies. He wishes to carve away at our trust so that we are no longer able to discern the true and trustworthy from the evil and manipulative.

Among the saddest realities of the church is that its leaders are just as susceptible to Satan's lies as anyone else. The church's earthly leaders often fall prey to Satan's lies, and the result is often the abuse of God's people. When pastors and other leaders of the church prove untrustworthy, God's people suffer, and Satan uses the opportunity to create a domino effect of distrust: if we cannot trust the people who are supposed to be God's representatives, then perhaps we cannot trust God Himself.

We must take particular care of those who have been hurt and abused by the church. We cannot blame them. We cannot shame them. And perhaps most difficult for us today, we cannot pretend like their experience was some rare and isolated incident. We must confess that we have a problem. Satan has infiltrated our churches and brought about ruin through his lies. We have believed those lies. We must be very careful when caring for those abused by the church to not manipulate them, to not run about saying, "Not all churches are like that." Or "I thank You, God, that we are not like other churches." We must mourn with those who mourn. We must repent. We must confess. We must work to protect God's people from abuse. We must work to discover and discern the lies of Satan when they come out of the mouths and pens of our leaders.

Also, if we cannot trust God, then how could we ever trust anyone else? One of the devil's secondary goals with this lie is to convince us that we cannot trust anything or anyone, leaving us isolated with nowhere to place our trust or our faith, convinced that there is nothing worth believing in at all.

The poisoned fruit of this lie might decay into loneliness, meaninglessness, hopelessness, despair. We hear Satan whisper, "God has abandoned you. Everyone has abandoned you. Life is pointless. Just give up." Such lies are the branches that shoot forth from the poisoned vine of Satan and his favorite lie: You cannot trust God.

THE TRUTH

The truth is we can trust God. God keeps His promises. Before God calls on the people of Israel to place their trust in Him as their God in the First Commandment, He speaks this Word: "I am the LORD your God, who brought you out of the land of Egypt, out of the house of slavery" (Exodus 20:2). God is saying to His people, "You can trust Me. I am your God. I brought you out of that suffering. Here are My Words, Words you can trust and live by."

When Satan tempts Jesus in Matthew 4, notice how Jesus responds: "It is written, 'Man shall not live by bread alone, but by every word that comes from the mouth of God'" (v. 4). This is such a brilliant answer. Jesus proclaims a truth etched in the Scriptures. But Jesus is also pointing back to His Baptism. A word has just come from the very mouth of God. The heavens were opened for all to hear this Word. Jesus is sustained by that living and active Word of God through forty days of fasting and through the accusations and temptations of Satan.

The truth is that we can trust God and His Word. As Psalm 18:30 says, "The word of the LORD proves true." Even when Satan manages to convince us to momentarily distrust God, God's Word proves true. It does not waver or falter.

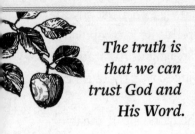

> *The truth is that we can trust God and His Word.*

God does not deceive or trick us. He seeks to establish an everlasting relationship with us. He creates us. He initiates the relationship. He remains committed to the relationship even when we do the most foolish things to damage our relationship with Him.

GOD'S DESIRED OUTCOME

While Satan's desired outcome is our distance from God and silence toward God, God's desired outcome is our nearness to Him. God's desired outcome is our constant communication with Him through prayer and meditation on His Word. As Paul writes, "Pray without ceasing" (1 Thessalonians 5:17).

While Satan desires our complete isolation, God desires our unity and our gathering in community and praise with others. While Satan desires our hopelessness, God desires to instill us with hope. While Satan desires meaninglessness in our lives, God desires to bring us into the fullness of abundant life through Jesus. As Jesus Himself says, "The thief comes only to steal and kill and destroy. I came that they may have life and have it abundantly" (John 10:10).

THE LOVE THAT CASTS OUT FEAR

The apostle John writes, "Perfect love casts out fear" (1 John 4:18). Dear reader, you are loved with the perfect love of Jesus. May His perfect love cast out the fear that Satan has planted in your life.

Satan wants you to be terrified of being wrong, to worry that one mistake will lead to your eternal damnation. Jesus took on that burden for you. Jesus entered into our humanity and endured the temptations of Satan without sin. Jesus was never wrong. Jesus is never wrong. Jesus will never be wrong. God raised Jesus from the dead, and this is what Jesus says to us: "As the Father has loved Me, so have I loved you. Abide in My love" (John 15:9).

Jesus loves you. Abide in that love. Bask in it. It is yours, even when you make mistakes, even when you are wrong. May Jesus' perfect love cast out any fear you have of being wrong.

Questions for Reflection

Where do you see this lie appearing in your life?

In what situations do you find it most difficult to trust God?

Can you remember a time when you were afraid of being wrong? What was that like?

Whom can you trust to tell you the truth when you are struggling with this lie?

Can you think of other biblical characters who struggle to trust God?

Scripture for Meditation

Proverbs 3:5–6

Isaiah 55:11

Ephesians 2:8–10

Matthew 13:1–23

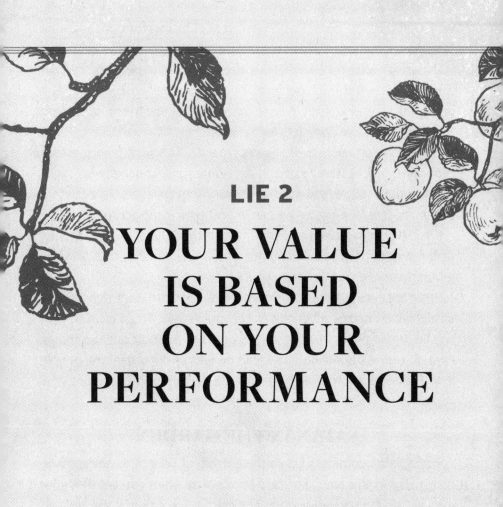

LIE 2

YOUR VALUE
IS BASED
ON YOUR
PERFORMANCE

What makes a person valuable? As we read this chapter's lie, we may very well think to ourselves, "Well, yeah. Our performance is what determines our value. That's true." After all, the world of work is filled with performance reviews that are often attached to people's compensation. The better your performance, the higher your value to the company or organization. We see this with athletes, the most successful of whom receive contracts for hundreds of millions of dollars. These contracts are offered based on performance. The more points, assists, rebounds, blocks, steals, strikeouts, home runs, touchdowns, sacks, interceptions, goals, saves, or whatever other measurable statistic a player records, the higher we can expect their contract to be.

If you have coworkers and you find out that one of them is getting paid more than you, you might be upset if you perceive that person's job performance is inferior to yours.

There are realms in our world where our performance rightly plays a role, which makes it difficult to recognize what Satan is up to with this lie. As we begin this chapter, I would like to point out two things. First, in our relationships, we are in danger of dehumanizing people if we reduce them to their performance. Second, God does not view you or value you according to your performance.

SATAN IN THE GARDEN

When Satan comes to Eve in the Garden of Eden, this chapter's lie is revealed in this line: "For God knows that when you eat of it your eyes will be opened, and you will be like God, knowing good and evil" (Genesis 3:5).

Who is the agent who must act to improve value? "You." Eve must do it herself. "God knows that when *you* eat of it *your* eyes will be opened, and *you* will be like God." Eve's value will increase to be like God's if she performs this one task. That is the lie Satan tells her.

English translations do not show us this immediately, but the "you" Satan uses in Genesis 3:1–5 is plural. Eve and Adam must do this themselves. They will be like God together. But they have to eat to have their eyes opened. Part of Eve's performance grade will be judged on getting Adam to join her in eating the fruit.

In this lie, Satan introduces a concept that is entirely foreign to a perfect creation—scarcity. In the perfect, abundant, evergreen Garden of Eden, Satan makes it seem like two perfect people are lacking. Like they need to do more. Like they need to have more. Like they can attain the things they are lacking through their own actions and performance.

> *Satan introduces a concept that is entirely foreign to a perfect creation—scarcity.*

Satan invents a problem and then points God's people inward to find the solution.

SATAN'S DESIRED OUTCOME

Satan loves this lie because it turns us in all sorts of directions, each away from God.

Through this lie, Satan seeks to curve human beings in on themselves. Satan wants us so concerned with our own value as judged by our performance that we do not care what God has to say about us. Satan does not want us to care about what our neighbors need (unless we can get something out of it). Satan wants everything we do to be for the sake of an improved self-image that seeks its identity away from the One in whose image we were made. Satan knows the stable, loving identity we possess as God's people. Satan wants us to abandon that certainty and seek our identity and validation elsewhere.

When we believe our value is based on our performance, our care for others might be driven by two unhelpful motivations: first, for the sake of competition and comparison, and second, for the sake of validation and admiration.

This lie simultaneously turns other people into tools to be used and problems to be conquered. It divorces us from our relationships and communities by turning our concerns ever inward and our problems ever outward.

Satan's lie makes us look inward to improve our circumstances rather than to God. It also tricks us into looking at others through the lens of comparison for validation (that we are doing better than them) or motivation (that we need to do better) rather than turning toward God and looking to Him for our value and validation.

Moreover, as Satan grows the branches of this lie, he convinces us to blame others for not giving us proper validation, for not noticing how hard we are working. And this lie persuades us to just try harder so that the world will be forced to notice us and value us. How painful is it when you feel disregarded? How much do you resent being made to feel small and insignificant? Satan amplifies these feelings so that we seek a constant diet of instant gratification.

If you believe your value is based on your performance, you will feel insatiable pressure to keep trying harder. Nothing will be good enough. You will ever be chasing a better possible performance (because we are not perfect). You will fix your eyes on the mirage of having a higher value than you have already been given in Jesus.

> *In one motion, Satan steers us away from God and away from our neighbor.*

In one motion, Satan steers us away from God and away from our neighbor. Our actions are not done because our neighbors need them. Our actions are not done out of service and love for God or neighbor. When Satan has his way, our actions are performed only for admiration. Our performance is only for praise. And no amount of praise will ever be enough to satiate and satisfy us. We will always want more (which moves us to Lie 3).

Our actual performance takes a back seat to how others perceive us and our performance. In this way, Satan's lie is not only "Your value is based on your performance" but, more sinisterly, "Your value is based on the admiration and praise of others."

Ultimately, every lie Satan tells festers with the desire that his coconspirators—sin and death—will flourish in the wake of the lie. Satan is like an anti–John the Baptist. When asked who he is, John the Baptist says of himself, "I am the voice of one crying out in the wilderness, 'Make straight the way of the Lord,' as the prophet Isaiah said" (John 1:23).

While John prepares the way of the Lord, Satan prepares the way for sin and death to come. He makes their paths straight and smooth. Satan seeks to make Jesus' path as crooked, rugged, and dangerous as possible.

Satan's desired outcome by telling us that our value is based on our performance is to get us to sin to gain people's praise and to get us to despair when that praise is absent.

Satan wants us to place the meaning in our lives in the wrong things because when those things are inevitably taken away, meaninglessness and hopelessness are quickly at hand.

THE FEAR BEHIND THE LIE

The fear I see lurking behind this lie is that we are not valued or admired. At the extreme, we fear we are worthless. We desperately want to know that we have value. We want that validation. We struggle so much in relationships when we work and strive and push and do our absolute best only to be treated with criticism, contempt, or—perhaps worst of all—indifference. We want to know that we matter. We want to know that we have value. When we are constantly doing things, constantly performing, constantly in the spotlight for people to see us and admire us and praise us, we long for such feedback to tell us we are valuable.

This fear and this lie are at the center of many broken relationships and marriages. When one spouse finds their performance at home is unappreciated and unvalued, they may spend more time elsewhere. Perhaps they log more hours at work because they can see their value there in the form of more money, productivity, or praise. Perhaps they spend more time with friends who more readily show approval of performance in the form of laughter, smiles, and jokes. Perhaps Satan moves such a spouse to spend time cultivating an inappropriate intimate relationship with someone else, where their performance as a romantic partner is more appreciated.

> *Part of Satan's strategy is to use lies and fears to create chaotic, tenuous situations that lead us to extreme, yet opposite, reactions.*

The fear of not being valued or admired might lead us to resent those who do not show us admiration. Or it may lead in the opposite direction of people pleasing, fawning over those who do admire us.

We see in this lie (as we will see in many others) that part of Satan's strategy is to use lies and fears to create chaotic, tenuous situations that lead us to extreme, yet opposite, reactions. We fawn, and we resent. We become workaholics, and we give up. We think we are absolutely brilliant, and we are convinced we are worthless. Satan wants us at these extremes because, at these extremes, we are curved in on ourselves more and more. At these extremes, we are made more impatient, more arrogant, more demanding, more fearful, and more susceptible to more lies.

Satan loathes any sense of humility or love. Satan seeks to block any possibility of patience, gentleness, or self-control. Any time we exhibit the fruit of the Spirit, as Paul describes in Galatians 5:22–23, Satan is enraged. He wants to poison us through fear of being worthless to produce the opposite of this fruit.

THE LIE REPEATED IN THE BIBLE

MEPHIBOSHETH

In 2 Samuel 9, King David asks a strange question. He asks whether any of King Saul's descendants are alive so that he can show them kindness. For years, Saul had tried to kill David and remove him from the conversation of who was the one, true king of Israel. But in the end, Saul dies, and David reigns. You would think that if a king were asking about the descendants of his rival, he might be asking with violent intent to secure his claim to the throne. But no. David wants to show kindness for the sake of Saul's son Jonathan, who was David's closest friend.

Enter Mephibosheth, Saul's grandson, Jonathan's son, and the heir to all that belongs to Saul. An accident in childhood had left Mephibosheth lame in both feet. As Mephibosheth comes before King David, the king tells him, "Do not fear, for I will show you kindness for the sake of your father Jonathan, and I will restore to you all the land of Saul your father, and you shall eat at my table always" (2 Samuel 9:7). Mephibosheth responds, "What is your servant, that you should show regard for a dead dog such as I?" (v. 8).

We do not know much about Mephibosheth. Perhaps he is simply being humble and self-deprecating before the king. But based on his words alone, it seems as though Mephibosheth sees himself as a dead dog, worthless, lacking in value. Perhaps this is because of his disability, perhaps it is because of living a life in squalor, perhaps it is because his family has all died. Regardless of why, calling oneself a dead dog communicates quite a negative feeling about oneself.

King David shows Mephibosheth an extreme kindness, adopting him into his royal family, treating him as an equal. Who knows what kind of lies Mephibosheth had been told by others? Who knows what lies

Satan had whispered in Mephibosheth's ears, convincing him of his utter worthlessness?

But this young man's value is not based on anything he can do. He is not shown kindness because he provides armies or gold or land to the king. Indeed, King David is the giver of all things and Mephibosheth the recipient, entirely and totally. He is shown kindness because David chooses to do so. Mephibosheth is prized, valued, loved, fed, cared for, and adopted into the family without any merit or worthiness in himself coming into the equation. It is all given, not earned. It is all gift, not wage.

Like Mephibosheth, we find that our place at King Jesus' table is not based on what we can give to Him, not earned by our performance. Our place is made possible only by Jesus' performance, by Jesus' love, by Jesus' kindness.

> *Our place at King Jesus' table is not based on what we can give to Him, not earned by our performance.*

SIMON PETER DENIES JESUS

On the day before Jesus dies, He celebrates the Passover with His disciples. As the meal concludes, a dispute arises among His disciples over who is to be regarded as the greatest. This is not the first time this conversation has occurred. Apparently, there was some competition among Jesus' followers. Jesus stops this conversation, saying, "Let the greatest among you become as the youngest, and the leader as one who serves. For who is the greater, one who reclines at table or one who serves? Is it not the one who reclines at table? But I am among you as the one who serves" (Luke 22:26–27). Jesus points them to humility and service, not greatness and performance.

Immediately after this conversation about greatness and service, Jesus says to Simon Peter, "Simon, Simon, behold, Satan demanded to have you, that he might sift you like wheat, but I have prayed for you that your faith may not fail. And when you have turned again, strengthen your brothers" (vv. 31–32). Then Peter replies, "Lord, I am ready to go with You both to prison and to death" (v. 33).

In Matthew's account, Peter singles himself out here and says, "Though they all fall away because of You, I will never fall away" (Matthew 26:33). Peter wants to be great in this regard. He wants his performance of faithfulness to be better than everyone else's.

But Jesus tells Peter the rock-hard truth: "Truly, I tell you, this very night, before the rooster crows, you will deny Me three times" (v. 34).

Satan demands to have Peter. We do not know what this looks like, but I am reminded of the opening chapters of the book of Job, as Satan seeks to assault Job. It seems Satan seeks to assault Simon Peter as well. We can see from Jesus' comment that what will follow in Peter's failure and denial of Jesus will be prompted by Satan.

Peter talks a big game. He can feel the trajectory of where things are headed. Simon Peter says he is ready to go with Jesus both to prison and to death. Yet that is not what happens, at least not until later for Simon Peter. What we say and even believe about ourselves is not always accurate. Sometimes our true identity is hidden from us.

Jesus and His disciples go out to pray on the Mount of Olives in a place called Gethsemane. Jesus takes Peter, James, and John with Him a bit further but then leaves them behind as well and goes off by Himself to pray. When Jesus returns, He finds His disciples sleeping. Here, Jesus singles out Peter, saying to him, "So, could you not watch with Me one hour? Watch

What we say and even believe about ourselves is not always accurate.

and pray that you may not enter into temptation. The spirit indeed is willing, but the flesh is weak" (vv. 40–41).

The temptation to deny Jesus is crouching at the door for Simon Peter. When Judas arrives with a collection of soldiers, Peter is the one who takes up a sword and cuts off the right ear of Malchus, servant of the high priest.[6]

Peter chooses violence over prison and death. Then Peter chooses to flee along with the rest of Jesus' disciples, just as Jesus had predicted and prophesied.

Some performance from Peter so far. Peter follows Jesus to the house of Caiaphas, where Jesus is on trial. And there, Peter denies Jesus three times. On the third denial, Luke records a detail that is so heartbreaking:

> But Peter said, "Man, I do not know what you are talking about." And immediately, while he was still speaking, the rooster crowed. And *the Lord turned and looked at Peter.* And Peter remembered the saying of the Lord, how He had said to him, "Before the rooster crows today, you will deny Me three times." And he went out and wept bitterly. (Luke 22:60–62, emphasis added)

Jesus can see Peter from inside the house. Jesus turns and looks at Peter. Imagine the look on His face.

Peter insisted he would not fall away or deny Jesus, but he did. His performance was a complete failure. And as Peter looks into the Lord's eyes and remembers their conversation, he weeps bitterly. He grieves his failure. He grieves his sin. But as we will see below, Peter is not defined by his performance.

---

6   John tells us the injured servant's name was Malchus and that it was Peter who wielded the sword (John 18:10–11). John and Luke both reveal it was the right ear. Luke is the only account that mentions Jesus actually healing Malchus (Luke 22:49–51). Matthew and Mark record the scene without all the details (Matthew 26:51–54; Mark 14:47–48).

THE LIE REPEATED IN OUR WORLD

The danger of this lie appears very early on in our lives. Some schools or families reward or punish kids for their performance in school. Good grades are rewarded with cash or a special occasion. Poor grades might mean being grounded. I would suggest such rewards and punishments for school performance be considered carefully.

Rewards and punishments affect relationships with those giving and receiving them. Every time people receive a reward or punishment for their performance, this lie seeks to infiltrate relationships where it does not belong. Satan does not play fair. Satan has no scruples. Satan will and does tempt children to believe that their value to their parents is based on their performance, that if they do not behave just so and perform at a certain level, their parents will stop loving them. The terror that might envelop a straight-A child who has a B-plus on a report card is very real. And that piece of identity does not go away easily. The feelings of inadequacy that arise in the straight-A graduate student with a B-plus on a transcript can be just as traumatic. Moreover, the student with the hard-earned C-minus average might face years of comparative devaluing.

When we are deceived by the lie that our value comes from our performance, we become more susceptible to applying that lie to other people and relationships. We may wrongly value our friends and family based on their usefulness to us. We may wrongly value fellow Christians based on how much time, energy, and money they give to the church. But the economy of the church is not in what we produce or how we perform. The economy of the church is entirely one way. Our value is based only and ever on our identity in Jesus. The eight-month-old who cries through every sermon is of just as much value as the pastor delivering that sermon. The adult with disabilities is of just as much value as the head trustee. The family that comes only on Easter is of just as much value as the family present every Sunday.

The preschooler who tears down a Christmas ornament is of just as much value as the altar guild member who designed, made, and placed said ornament.

Our value is based only and ever on our identity in Jesus.

As Paul writes, "For in Christ Jesus you are all sons of God, through faith. For as many of you as were baptized into Christ have put on Christ. There is neither Jew nor Greek, there is neither slave nor free, there is no male and female, for you are all one in Christ Jesus" (Galatians 3:26–28). Our identity comes from Baptism into Jesus. Our value comes not from the name we are called in Baptism but from the name that we are baptized into—the name of the Father and of the Son and of the Holy Spirit. This name, which also begins every worship service, marks each of us as a valued child of God, equally priceless in His sight.

Adding to the challenge of this lie is the fact that our standards are often arbitrary, subjective, and unspecified. Consider how quickly sports fans turn on a player who performs poorly. After drafting Russell Wilson for my 2022 fantasy football team and watching an abysmal performance unravel week after week, I turned on him. I will never draft him again, even if he is named the Most Valuable Player in the league in a subsequent season. I judge him based on performance, because his only value to me is as a fantasy football player.

But how often do we treat our real-life relationships like a fantasy football lineup? How often do we hand out grades in our mind to our friends, coworkers, parishioners, kids, or spouse? A friend who does not text back quickly enough (a time frame we have invented without anyone's knowledge and enforce with wild inconsistencies) gets benched to being an acquaintance pretty quickly. If they want to get back into the starting friend lineup, they must earn it. *They* must reach out. A spouse with a lengthening list of to-dos gets a D and the threat of failure if performance doesn't improve.

When we judge the people in our life based on performance, we may experience and assume they do the same to us. We might wrongly extend this assumption toward God, believing that He judges us based on our performance. So, to make things fair, we return the judgment back on God. We judge God based on His performance. We use the ease and extravagance of our lives as the measuring stick by which we grade God's performance. If our lives are full of comforts and riches while lacking in drama and difficulty, we give God an A. However, if we are suffering, if we meet a challenge that we cannot overcome, if we meet unfairness of any kind, well, then God's grades start slipping. The car breaking down drops God to a B-plus. An unfavorable health diagnosis brings God down to a C-minus. A death in the family might put God on academic probation.

Perhaps you are familiar with the concept of prosperity gospel, the false notion that the more faithful we are (especially in the area of stewardship), the more God will bless us with material wealth. Prosperity gospel is rooted in this very lie: your value is based on your performance. The logic of prosperity gospel is that the only way out of suffering and challenges is to further burden oneself, swallowing lies such as "If I had more faith, God wouldn't do this to me."

But when it comes to our grading of God, we have created a kind of prosperity faith, a conditional faith that seeks to hold God hostage if He doesn't meet our demands. As we do this, we seek to transform our relationship with God into the opposite of prosperity gospel. Instead of us needing to meet God's demands, it is God who must meet our demands.

> *We have created a kind of prosperity faith, a conditional faith that seeks to hold God hostage if He doesn't meet our demands.*

We seek to claim the role and control of God. We mutiny. We seize control. (We will visit the seizure of control more with Lie 4.)

But both are false gospels. Both are lies. Prosperity gospel is a lie. God has made no promise to continually reward us with more and more money. There are faithful people who are quite wealthy and faithful people who have nothing. Possessing wealth is not a problem; nor is it a sign that God approves of all your actions. Our work in the kingdom of God is not based on commission, as if the world were a used car lot and we were all salespeople.

But our mutiny of God, to try to overtake His role and demand His performance improve to make our lives easier, that is also false and completely impossible. We cannot hold God hostage.

THE TRUTH

Your value is based on God's love. Your value is based on Christ's actions of death and resurrection for you. Your value is based on Jesus' performance for you. Your value is given as a gift. You cannot change your value to God. You are His pearl of great price. He has given everything so that you can be His own.

Though Satan prepares the way for sin and death, we are called like John the Baptist to prepare the way for Jesus to arrive. We prepare the way for Jesus to forgive sin. We prepare the way for Jesus to give new life. We prepare the way for Jesus to do His work in the lives of others by pointing them to Jesus and the gifts of His work.

If you look to yourself and your own performance for any assurance, you either risk pretending you are better than you truly are or risk despairing at the reality of how poor your performance is compared with the perfection required for salvation.

Paying attention to your performance is helpful only insofar as it drives you back to God's grace and mercy.

After Jesus rises from the dead, He appears to His followers on several occasions. On one of those occasions, Jesus takes Peter aside and asks him, "Simon, son of John, do you love Me?" (John 21:16). Jesus asks this three times. This seems quite intentional—once for every time Peter denied Jesus. John tells us that "Peter was grieved because He said to him the third time, 'Do you love Me?'" (v. 17). But Peter is not defined by his denial of Jesus. Peter is restored and called on to go and feed Jesus' sheep, to follow Jesus once again. Peter is not restored because of his abysmal performance; Peter is restored because of Jesus' mercy and His victory over death and the grave.

> *Paying attention to your performance is helpful only insofar as it drives you back to God's grace and mercy.*

So, too, our restoration and forgiveness is not based on our past, present, or future performance. It is only ever based on Jesus and His love for us, His performance of death and resurrection.

GOD'S DESIRED OUTCOME

God's desired outcome is that we find our value in Jesus. God brings this outcome about in many ways. Some of us begin to learn our value is in Jesus through a series of massive personal failures that force us to realize our own performance is pitiful. Some of us learn our value is in Jesus through the failure of relationships where we invested too much of our identity. Some of us learn our value is in Jesus through the unconditional love of another who had already learned the lesson. Any one of us who learns our value is in Jesus ultimately learns this because the Holy Spirit calls us by the Gospel, the Gospel of Jesus' love for us shown in His incarnation, death, and resurrection. Jesus values us so highly that He chooses to leave the heavens and come down into this world of suffering. He chooses to take on not only our humanity but also our very sin. He takes our sin to the cross and crucifies it there. He lays our sin down, dead in the tomb with Him.

And then He rises from the dead, but our sin remains forever parted from us. We are forgiven. That is how much Jesus values you. He willingly dies for you. He gives His life for yours.

> *He rises from the dead, but our sin remains forever parted from us. We are forgiven.*

Jesus goes to great lengths in the desire that we find our identity, security, meaning, and value in Him.

And when we do, our performance is then liberated from any hope of increased value or fear of decreased value before God. Our actions in the world can then be rightly directed toward our neighbors in unconditional love.

THE LOVE THAT CASTS OUT FEAR

God created the world and filled it with abundant life. He loves all His creation purely because it is His. He made it. Yes, God's good creation fell into sin, but God did not require the creation to save itself. God did not require Adam and Eve to save themselves. God sent Jesus to save Adam, Eve, all humanity, and all creation. Why? Because He loves us. Because our value to Him is not based on our performance; our value is determined by His love for us.

In his theses for the Heidelberg Disputation, Luther writes, "The love of God does not find, but creates, that which is pleasing to it."[7] The love of God does not judge us based on how deserving we are of love. The love of God creates and re-creates us, forms and transforms us.

You need not fear that you are not valued or admired. You are God's preoccupation. You are His absolute delight. He has found you. Forgiven you. Re-created you. Transformed you. Would God really do all that if He did not value you? These actions are clear evidence of His love for you and of how much He values you.

---

7 *Luther's Works*, volume 31, p. 41.

Questions for Reflection

Where do you see this lie appearing in your life?

In what areas of life do you tend to care most about your performance?

Can you remember a time when you were afraid you were not valued? What was that like?

Whom can you trust to tell you the truth when you are struggling with this lie?

Can you think of other biblical characters whose identity was wrapped up in their accomplishments?

Scripture for Meditation

Matthew 6:25–34

Matthew 10:29–31

1 John 3:1–3

Psalm 25

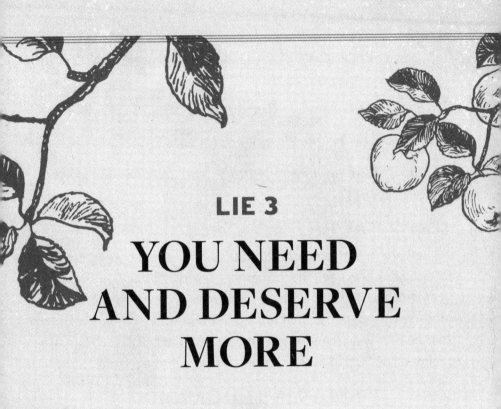

LIE 3

YOU NEED AND DESERVE MORE

If you own a television, smartphone, or computer, you are inundated with this message every single day. Nearly every advertisement relies on the premise that we need more stuff. And we deserve that stuff. Just consider some of the ubiquitous taglines major corporations have used over the years:

"Have it your way." —*Burger King*

"Because you're worth it." —*L'Oreal*

"Double your pleasure. Double your fun." —*Wrigley's Doublemint Gum*

"Expect More. Pay Less." —*Target*

Whether it is in their slogan or not, advertisers are banking on you believing that you need more, that you deserve more.

I am not accusing any of these companies of being evil. Their livelihood depends on people purchasing their products. They simply know that the best way to get people to purchase their stuff is to tap into the insatiable human desire that we all have for more, more, more.

SATAN IN THE GARDEN

Satan seeks to create this desire for more within Eve in Genesis 3. Satan advertises the tree of the knowledge of good and evil as a means to more. Satan says, "For God knows that when you eat of it your eyes will be opened, and you will be like God, knowing good and evil" (Genesis 3:5). Of course, this is true. Eve's eyes will be opened. She will know both good and evil. She will be like God in that one particular way. And she currently is not like God in that one particular way, so she is missing out. There is more to be had, and that more is so easily accessible. Just do it, Eve.

Why would Eve go through life without this? It is so easily obtained. And back to Lie 1, why would God withhold this from Eve? Clearly, she cannot trust God if He is withholding something, especially something that will help her be more like God.

As we have noted already, the problem is that in becoming more like God in this one way, Eve will lose her likeness to God in many other ways. She will not be perfect or holy any longer. She will not be sinless any longer. Before the fall, Eve knows only good, but now she will know evil, for she will have listened to and participated in the evil of disobedience.

The advertising slogan "You will be like God" turns out to be both true and false. Likewise, Target's "Expect More. Pay Less." slogan might be true, but I am guessing you and I share the experience of going to Target for three things and walking out with a cartful. Even though the prices may have been competitive, we expected more and we paid more, not less, because we bought more than we needed.

SATAN'S DESIRED OUTCOME

Satan's desired outcome with this lie is that we are never satisfied, that we consume and devour as much as we possibly can. Satan hopes we will be envious, jealous, and covetous. Satan wants us to be in a perpetual state of breaking the Tenth Commandment, coveting and being desirous of everything that belongs to our neighbors.

Satan hopes that we will look at what God has given us and dismiss it as not enough or not good enough. Satan's desire is that we take a good gift of God and demand more or demand something other than what we have.

> *Satan hopes that we will look at what God has given us and dismiss it as not enough or not good enough.*

Consider the other options Eve has in the Garden of Eden. She could eat from any other tree and find the most delicious fruit we can imagine. She could eat from the tree of life itself. She could enjoy any one of God's perfect gifts. But Satan convinces her that she needs something different, something more, something other than what God has given her. Satan persuades Eve that she needs what God has forbidden. Eve covets her heavenly Neighbor's fruit.

In this way, Satan seeks to move our desires out of alignment with God's desires. Then, Satan seeks to move our desires into alignment with his own evil desires. Satan seeks first to differentiate us from God, to make us feel independent of Him. If we are independent of God, then we can ignore God's desires. Once we are loosed from dependence on God (so the lie goes), then Satan suggests to us the disobedient desires he so loves, inviting us to claim such desires as our own.

Satan seeks to make God's people selfish, gluttonous, and addicted. Satan wants people who are unable to restrain themselves from anything they desire. Satan's desired outcome with this lie is to stir up as much discontentment as possible. Satan desires that our minds are filled with covetous thoughts, our mouths complain about how unfair everything is, and our feet carry us to claim whatever our hearts desire.

THE FEAR BEHIND THE LIE

The fear behind this lie is the fear of missing out, a fear of scarcity, a fear of being deprived. This is where advertisers are so good at their job. They show people enjoying their products and filled with so much joy and pleasure and satisfaction. We are terrified that we will miss out on such joys and pleasures, and here is the perfect product to ensure we will not miss out.

It is always interesting to watch TV shows and identify the target audience based solely on the advertisements. When I watch *The Price Is Right*, I see commercials for reverse mortgages, life insurance, and wheelchairs. When I watch football on a Sunday afternoon, I see commercials for beer, pizza, and pickup trucks.

Again, there is nothing wrong with seeing an advertisement and being persuaded to buy that product. That might be how you came to buy this very book. Advertisements are not evil, but they can be dangerous. Satan's tactic with the lie that we need and deserve more is to never let us feel like we have enough. Satan wants us fixated on the fear of being deprived and the pursuit of more.

For some people, the fear of being deprived has to do with the consumption of food and drink. For others, being deprived has to do with a lack of experiences and entertainment. The fear then may reveal itself as a fear of boredom or a fear of being left out of social situations. Whatever the case may be, Satan wants us focused on what we lack, not on what we have, not on the good gifts God has given us.

> *Satan wants us focused on what we lack, not on what we have, not on the good gifts God has given us.*

THE LIE REPEATED IN THE BIBLE

THE PARABLE OF THE WEDDING FEAST

Jesus tells this parable in Luke 14:8–11:

> When you are invited by someone to a wedding feast, do not sit down in a place of honor, lest someone more distinguished than you be invited by him, and he who invited you both will come and say to you, "Give your place to this person," and then you will begin with shame to take the lowest place. But when you are invited, go and sit in the lowest place, so that when your host comes he may say to you, "Friend, move up higher." Then you will be honored in the presence of all who sit at table with you. For everyone who exalts

himself will be humbled, and he who humbles himself
will be exalted.

This way of thinking sounds terribly foreign in a world that tells us to grab life by the horns, to pull ourselves up by our bootstraps, to take what we want because nobody is going to give us anything.

It sounded foreign in Jesus' day as well. One of the things people in Jesus' day wanted more and more of was prestige. People wanted to appear as though they were the most important, the most honorable. Even Jesus' disciples argue about who is the greatest among them. But Jesus warns several times in His teachings and parables against such seeking of prestige.

Jesus gives this warning about the scribes and pharisees:

> They do all their deeds to be seen by others. For they make their phylacteries broad and their fringes long,[8] and they love the place of honor at feasts and the best seats in the synagogues and greetings in the market-places and being called rabbi by others. But you are not to be called rabbi, for you have one teacher, and you are all brothers. And call no man your father on earth, for you have one Father, who is in heaven. Neither be called instructors, for you have one instructor, the Christ. The greatest among you shall be your servant. Whoever exalts himself will be humbled, and whoever humbles himself will be exalted. (Matthew 23:5–12)

The scribes and pharisees were constantly showing off with their clothes, their greetings, their giving, everything. They were constantly exalting themselves as high as possible. They wanted more and more exalting. They believed Satan's lie that they needed more, that they deserved more. But Jesus' words to these powerful religious leaders echo through time and space to us and to our religious leaders:

---

8   This is a description of the clothes religious leaders wore in Jesus' day to show off their positions.

"Whoever exalts himself will be humbled, and whoever humbles himself will be exalted" (v. 12).

Jesus shows again and again that in His kingdom the first are last and the last are first. He shows us that the greatest in the kingdom of heaven is not the most powerful but the most helpless, like children.

Jesus shows again and again that in His kingdom the first are last and the last are first.

THE PARABLE OF THE WORKERS IN THE VINEYARD

One story Jesus tells is about a vineyard owner who goes out and hires servants to work in his vineyard. The owner goes out at sunrise, as would have been customary, and hires as many people as he can for the typical day's wage: one denarius.[9] But the vineyard owner sees there is much more work to do, so he keeps going back to the marketplace and finding people standing idle with no work to do. He hires them to go work in his vineyard as well; as far as wage expectations, he tells them, "Whatever is right I will give you" (Matthew 20:4). The vineyard owner does this several times, hiring people at five different times throughout the day.

When the day is over and it is time for the laborers to be paid, he invites those who had worked only one hour to come forward and receive their pay. It was a twelve-hour day, and the laborers who had worked the full twelve hours had agreed on a denarius for the day, so we would expect these latecomers to receive one-twelfth of a denarius, at most. But those who had worked one hour receive a whole denarius. They receive twelve times their expected wage. Everybody in line who had worked three hours, six hours, nine hours, or twelve hours starts doing the math in their head, hopeful of receiving more.

---

9   I live about an hour away from the Napa Valley. Seasonal harvest workers in Napa Valley vineyards make $20–$28 per hour. For a twelve-hour day, that would mean $240–$336 in today's value.

But as they come forward, each receives a denarius. Those who had worked only part of a day do not complain. They are receiving more than they should have, even if it is proportionally less than those who had worked only one hour. But the laborers who had worked a full twelve-hour day are upset and say so. They grumble, saying, "These last worked only one hour, and you have made them equal to us who have borne the burden of the day and the scorching heat" (v. 12). These laborers believe they deserve more. They are insulted by being made equal to people who had worked only one hour.

But the vineyard owner speaks a straightforward truth to them: "Friend, I am doing you no wrong. Did you not agree with me for a denarius? Take what belongs to you and go. I choose to give to this last worker as I give to you. Am I not allowed to do what I choose with what belongs to me? Or do you begrudge my generosity?" (vv. 13–15).

The laborers who grumble have believed the lie that they deserve more. They feel entitled to more of the vineyard owner's money. They receive exactly what was agreed on, yet they covet what they do not have. Everyone else receives what the vineyard owner promised by his own word—"whatever is right." The owner decided that what was right was to be generous to those who were hired last. The laborers would have divided the wages differently, but that was not their call to make.

They focus on what they lack, not on what they have.

Satan stirs up discontentment in the laborers who have worked all day, even though they receive exactly what was promised. They focus on what they lack, not on what they have.

In this parable, the vineyard owner stands in for our generous God. Satan's lie of "You deserve more" persuades the laborers to desire something other than what was promised by the generous Owner. They end up begrudging His generosity, which puts them in terrible danger of begrudging the Owner Himself. When the vineyard Owner comes calling for laborers the next day, how many of these laborers who worked all day will refuse to go into the vineyard for this Owner? How many will carry their begrudging discontentment with them? How many will fall for Satan's lie instead of being content in the Owner's promise?

THE LIE REPEATED IN OUR WORLD

We see this lie play out every day in ways that have become commonplace. We see a new phone is available, and we want it. We see a bigger, sharper TV is on sale, and we want it. We watch a new car drive by, and we want it. We see the lottery jackpot reach a certain point, and we cannot help but covet those millions of dollars and dream about what it would be like to have all that money.

There is nothing wrong with selling or purchasing a phone, TV, or car. The problem wriggles to life when we seek more from a product than it can deliver. When we look to a new car to satisfy a desire bigger than simply having a means of transportation, it cannot deliver. When we look to a phone as a means of belonging, it cannot deliver. When we try to purchase friends, prestige, or glory through the giant TV, it cannot deliver.

We may subconsciously look to such purchases for more than they can give, and we end up discontented. Whatever satisfaction we receive from purchasing anything is short-lived because a newer phone, a bigger TV, and a fancier car will be available in a matter of moments. The fear of missing out and the desire for more will return. We can never keep up with our own desires for more. Our ability to discern what we need and whether certain choices and purchases

> *We can never keep up with our own desires for more.*

are wise has been damaged by this lie, which Satan repeats with ever-increasing volume.

In my local grocery store, there have been several times when some item was in short supply. In the early part of the COVID-19 pandemic, it was toilet paper. People were limited to buying one package of toilet paper, and each day's shipment would sell out in a matter of minutes. For a while, flour was hard to come by because everybody was baking homemade bread. Then feta cheese was scarce, thanks to a phenomenon called TikTok pasta. Later, it was eggs. Shoppers were limited to two dozen eggs. I still have a hard time locating my wife's contact solution. Whenever I actually see it in a store, I am tempted to buy a year's supply.

The desire for more and more derives from a mindset of scarcity. We tell ourselves that there are only so many resources in the world, so we need to gather and hoard as many and as much as possible for ourselves. It is unlikely that you hoarded toilet paper before the COVID-19 pandemic. But if you saw some on the shelves in March or April of 2020, did you buy some even though you did not need it? The threat of scarcity drives us to hoard, to overspend, to do whatever it takes to not be caught without something.

Consider the pandemonium of Black Friday shopping. People have literally harmed others, shoving them out of the way, in order to get the item they want at the lowest price possible. Or consider the price tag on thirty seconds of advertising during the Super Bowl—more than $7 million for Super Bowl LVIII in 2024. There are only so many possible slots for advertising during the game. The limited availability to reach so many people drives up the price.

The threat of scarcity affects more than just the realm of material things. When we fear that power is scarce, we may risk everything we can to maintain it. (More on this in the next chapter.) We lie. We cheat. We steal. We lie about the cheating and stealing.

The church is not immune to this. In the church, the preservation of power has taken the form of nondisclosure agreements, outright abuse, veiled (or not-so-veiled) threats, and various political tactics that are unbecoming of Christ's church.

Sadly, when many in the church hear of such abuse, they respond with something like, "I thank You, God, that we are not like other churches," rather than searching for and exposing the lies and power abuses in their own midst.

We so often choose a pretend superiority, which is just another version of this lie. We pretend we are better than these other churches, these other Christians, so we deserve better too. We deserve more. We slip back to the previous lie of thinking our performance has earned us more.

On numerous occasions, I have watched the struggles of Christians from other traditions and caught myself thinking, "I hope these people will leave that church and join mine." And if I am honest with myself, my motivation in such a thought is tainted by this lie, by my own unsatiable desire for more.

Behind the desire for more is a desire for less. We hope for fewer obstacles and challenges in life. We often think that having more money and more stuff will bring about a life that is all ease and no drama, but that simply is not the case. When we actually receive the more we are looking for, we often find that it amplifies all the negatives we are trying to reduce. When a person comes into a lot of money, the lie "I deserve more" echoes out to every family member and friend; every acquaintance and neighbor thinks they deserve a slice of that person's success or luck.

Behind the desire for more is a desire for less.

One of the most profound and heartbreaking documentaries I have seen is called *Broke*. It's the story of how many professional athletes end up filing for bankruptcy. Families and friends often take advantage of athletes and their newfound wealth. Families are ruined. Friendships are destroyed. Athletes who had earned millions of dollars over the course of their careers—athletes who undoubtedly celebrated at the idea of more money, more security, more ease in life—are left with nothing.

Nowadays, people who win large lottery jackpots sometimes do not even reveal their identity. Some do not tell their own family members about the win. Because, like it or not, money changes relationships between people.

This lie can turn into "I need more so that I can say yes to everyone else who also needs more." But everyone else's desires are just as insatiable as our own. We can never have enough to make everyone happy.

THE TRUTH

The truth is we do not have to seek more and more, because our God is the Creator and Sustainer of the world. He has given us all that we need to support this body and life and still takes care of us. When Jesus teaches us the Lord's Prayer, He does not invite us to pray for more and more; rather, His invitation is to pray, "Give us this day our daily bread" (Matthew 6:11).

Shortly after this, Jesus says,

> Therefore do not be anxious, saying, "What shall we eat?" or "What shall we drink?" or "What shall we wear?" For the Gentiles seek after all these things, and your heavenly Father knows that you need them all. But seek first the kingdom of God and His righteousness, and all these things will be added to you. (vv. 31–33)

Jesus' invitation is to trust that God will take care of us, to be content with what we have, and not to seek after more and more and more. Whether we are seeking more money, more honor, more fame, or more power, Jesus tells us to stop. Jesus invites us to humble ourselves, to be dependent on God rather than to hoard as much as we can for ourselves.

A simultaneous truth is that many people in our world are poor and in need. Many people do not have reliable access to basic needs like clean water, food, and shelter.

When I was in college, I went to Peru to visit a friend who was serving as a missionary there. I remember visiting one particular woman in her home. Her home had dirt floors. The whole home was not much bigger than the size of the guest bedroom I'm sitting in right now. She hosted us and talked with us about what life was like. As we were about to leave, she told us she would pray for us. I reflexively responded, "Thank you. I'll pray for you too." But she stopped and said, "No. You don't understand. You have too much. I have nothing. I have to rely on God. You have too much. I will pray for you."

> *Jesus' invitation is to trust that God will take care of us.*

No one is exempt from this lie, but it seems increasingly dangerous the more material goods and comforts we actually have.

GOD'S DESIRED OUTCOME

God's desired outcome is that no matter how much we have, we trust Him more and more. At the end of Philippians, Paul says,

> **I have learned in whatever situation I am to be content. I know how to be brought low, and I know how to abound. In any and every circumstance, I have learned the secret of facing plenty and hunger,**

abundance and need. I can do all things through Him who strengthens me. (Philippians 4:11–13)

Depending on your own circumstances and experiences, it may be easy to understand how having very little would increase a person's trust in the Lord. Since the poor have very little, they cannot put their hope in anything but the Lord. But we may also find the opposite occurs. Having very little and being constantly in need may cause a person to trust the Lord less and less, to view the Lord with increasing distrust. Similar opposite outcomes can occur for those who have an abundance. Being wealthy is not an automatic condemnation to believing this lie. Many wealthy people are full of gratitude and frequently sacrifice much to help others. But the outcome may just as easily be that they constantly chase after more and more.

What does it look like to live faithfully when we have an abundance?

In an affluent culture, what does it look like to live faithfully when we have an abundance? How do we content ourselves when life is abundantly full with more than we need? How do we trust God more and more when we are quite comfortable?

Whether we have an abundance or are in need, our recognition of our relationship to God is vital. God is our Creator. We are His creations. God has given us all that we have. God can take away all that we have in a moment. God's desired outcome is that we recognize Him as the source of what we have. The money in our bank accounts, whether pennies or a portfolio of billions, came from God. He is the source. James writes, "Every good gift and every perfect gift is from above, coming down from the Father of lights, with whom there is no variation or shadow due to change" (James 1:17).

Likewise, Jesus invites us into this dependent relationship, saying,

> Ask, and it will be given to you; seek, and you will find; knock, and it will be opened to you. For everyone who asks receives, and the one who seeks finds, and to the one who knocks it will be opened. Or which one of you, if his son asks him for bread, will give him a stone? Or if he asks for a fish, will give him a serpent? If you then, who are evil, know how to give good gifts to your children, how much more will your Father who is in heaven give good things to those who ask Him! (Matthew 7:7–11)

God wants us to look to Him for all good. He wants us to ask for good things and trust that what we receive is truly best for us. He wants us to remember that we are His precious children. He wants us to live in the perpetual knowledge and comfort that nothing can separate us from the good gift of His love.

THE LOVE THAT CASTS OUT FEAR

Psalm 23 is perhaps the most beloved chapter in the Bible, and with good reason. Psalm 23 has a feeling of calm, a sense that all will be well even in the darkest, most dangerous situations. The opening verse says, "The LORD is my shepherd; I shall not want."

Since the Lord is our shepherd, we lack nothing. He leads us to the best pastures, where food, water, and safety abound. He walks with us through darkness, grief, even death itself. As King David writes, "Even though I walk through the valley of the shadow of death, I will fear no evil, for You are with me; Your rod and Your staff, they comfort me" (v. 4). God's presence casts out fear. We need not fear scarcity with Him. We need not fear missing out on what other people have, because we have the green pastures and still waters of Jesus. We are given an everlasting, unshakable kingdom. We are given the perfect Shepherd and King, who is risen from the dead with all authority in heaven and on earth. We can trust Him to bring us where we need to be, even when we cannot see how it all will work out.

We need not fear scarcity with Him.

Questions for Reflection

Where do you see this lie appearing in your life?

In what situations do you find it most difficult to be content?

Can you remember a time when you were afraid of missing out? What was that like?

Whom can you trust to tell you the truth when you are struggling with this lie?

Can you think of other biblical characters who struggle with always wanting more?

Scripture for Meditation

Psalm 23

Ephesians 3:14–21

Luke 11:1–13

LIE 4

LIFE WILL BE BETTER IF YOU SEIZE MORE CONTROL

When we believe the previous chapter's lie that we need and deserve more, Satan pushes us to take the next logical step: go get it. If we need and deserve more, then we should take action and seize what we need and deserve. The previous lie can encompass money and materials, fame and power. This lie also includes these facets of desire. It seems to me that money and materials are more central to Lie 3. The central focus of this lie is our desire for power.

SATAN IN THE GARDEN

As we covered in previous lies, one of the things Satan says to Eve is, "For God knows that when you eat of it your eyes will be opened, and you will be like God, knowing good and evil" (Genesis 3:5).

It is such a nefarious sentence because it is entirely true. Eating the fruit from the tree of the knowledge of good and evil will open Adam and Eve's eyes to know good and evil, to be like God in that one particular way. All that is true.

The unspoken implication is that this is good, that this new reality of knowing good and evil will be better than the paradise Adam and Eve currently enjoy. The lie is in the implication that God is not just withholding a perfectly tasty fruit but also withholding power from them, that God does not want them to be like Him.

> *Satan encourages Eve to assert control over her situation, to be the master of her own destiny.*

Satan's logic is that since God is holding out on Adam and Eve (even though He isn't) and since there is a better reality to be grasped and pulled down (even though there isn't), Eve should obviously go, take the fruit, eat, and enter that new and better life where she will be like God.

Satan encourages Eve to assert control over her situation, to be the master of her own destiny. Notice how this relates back to Lie 1.

Satan accuses God of not being trustworthy because He has withheld goodness from Adam and Eve. It is as if Satan is saying to Eve, "You're telling me that God put this tree right in front you, but then forbid you from eating it? How strange? And it's the tree in the middle of the garden? Just sitting there, tempting you all the time? And it contains knowledge? Well, knowledge is power! Clearly, God is holding out on you. Clearly, you need to seize control of this situation, and then things will improve."

So the logic goes: There's a perfectly good tree that will improve your life. God has forbidden it to keep you under His thumb. You cannot trust God. Rise up, take, eat, and you will have more. You will be like God, equal to God, out from under His tyrannical, untrustworthy rule.

SATAN IN THE WILDERNESS

When Jesus is in the wilderness, Satan twice tempts Him to seize power in some way. Satan comes to Jesus after He has been fasting in the wilderness for forty days. Jesus is hungry. So Satan offers a simple solution: "Command these stones to become loaves of bread" (Matthew 4:3). "It is easy, Jesus," Satan seems to say. "Seize more control over Your situation, and all will be well. Show Your power as the supposed Son of God." Later he tempts Jesus to be hungry for power. Satan shows Jesus all the kingdoms of the world and all their glory and says, "All these I will give You, if You will fall down and worship me" (Matthew 4:9).

Satan is playing chess with these temptations. In the first, Satan does not want Jesus to suffer the inconveniences of being human. Hunger is not a necessary thing to endure for the divine Son of God, for one with the power to transform stones into bread. Just create some food and stop being hungry. The nudge toward power and control here is not so much in showing off the power—after all, no one else is around—but rather in not enduring the inconvenience and limitations of being human. If Jesus is the Son of God, as God the Father has just proclaimed Him to be, then why not enjoy all the conveniences that power has to offer? Satan wants Jesus to forgo any human limitation.

I cannot be sure, but it seems to me that Satan is attempting to soften Jesus' resolve, to prepare Him to not endure other inconveniences that are surely coming His way. If Jesus can be persuaded to use His power to overcome the inconvenience of hunger, perhaps Jesus can be persuaded to use His power to overcome the inconvenience of the cross. If Jesus forgoes the inconvenience of hunger, perhaps He will forgo the much larger inconvenience of death.

Which is where the other temptation comes in. Jesus' mission is to bring the reign and rule of God to earth. We see in the rest of the book of Matthew what God's reign and rule looks like. As Jesus tells John the Baptist, "The blind receive their sight and the lame walk, lepers are cleansed and the deaf hear, and the dead are raised up, and the poor have good news preached to them" (Matthew 11:5).

Jesus brings restoration to everything Satan has broken. As Satan offers up all the kingdoms of the world, he is trying to persuade Jesus to take the easy way. The point and purpose of Jesus' incarnation (at least in part) is to reclaim these kingdoms of the world from Satan's power. Satan is offering them up without a fight. Whether Satan knows of Jesus' plan of suffering, death, and resurrection, I cannot say. Regardless of what Satan knows, he offers Jesus the path of least resistance. "You want these kingdoms? Go ahead. They are yours. No cross. No suffering. No struggle at all. Just worship me, and I'll hand them over."

Satan offers Jesus the opportunity to seize control of His own destiny, a chance for Him to avoid all the ugliness of human life and death. Satan sets himself up as a viable alternative to God. God's will and way requires pain and suffering, even death. Satan's way is much easier, the bending of a knee. Seize control and life will be better, easier. Of course, Jesus knows that such an action would upend the world in everlasting destruction, division, and violence. Jesus chooses ever-lasting righteousness, innocence, and blessedness.

SATAN'S DESIRED OUTCOME

Satan loves this lie in part because he believes it is the truth. Satan lives out this lie in everything he does. Satan seeks to seize control away from God. And Satan wants us to follow him, to emulate him in

Jesus chooses everlasting righteousness, innocence, and blessedness.

the unquenchable quest for power and glory and control. Satan's desired outcome is for us to be less and less like God and more and more like Satan, to be made in his demonic image: an insatiably power-hungry tyrant.

Another part of the reason why Satan loves this particular lie is that he can twist its opposite into just as painful of a lie. As God's people, we recognize God's position as the Creator, Sustainer, and Savior of the world. We are called to let God remain in His position as God and take our rightful places as His creations who receive every good gift from His hand. As God's creatures, we receive responsibilities and voca-tions from Him. When we reject this lie, when we refuse to seize power, Satan tempts us toward the other extreme. Satan tries to get us to abdicate all our responsibilities. Satan does this by showing us just how little power we have. He puts us in helpless situations, pulling us toward despair and meaningless-ness. Like with previous lies, Satan wants us at the extremes. Either we emulate him as power-hungry

Satan wants us at the extremes. Either we emulate him as power-hungry tyrants or we fall into despair over how little power we have.

tyrants or we fall into despair over how little power we have and get trampled by those who have decided to seek and claim power.

THE FEAR BEHIND THE LIE

A combination of fears are at play with this lie. Sometimes we seize control because we fear being controlled by others. We fear being manipulated or used by others. Someone has to have power and be in control. We believe others will treat us like pawns, so we take control ourselves. We tell ourselves that the only way to avoid being taken advantage of is to control everything ourselves. In so doing, we often miss how we are taking advantage of others, how we are manipulating them and treating them as inferior. We might fail to acknowledge that we are just as untrustworthy as anyone else.

But we also may be driven to seize more control because it helps us with other lies. It is easier to cover up one's sins and mistakes (see Lie 6) from a position of power. We may fear losing our power because of a lingering feeling that we have built a house of cards that could topple at any moment. We catastrophize and think our entire lives are going to fall apart if we are not maneuvering and manipulating every little thing. We are afraid, perhaps, that Lie 1 and Lie 2 are true, that we are defined by our performance (and we know we have been fudging the numbers) and that we cannot trust God or anyone else to catch us if our house of cards starts to fall. We are afraid of being weak and powerless, so we grab more power. We are afraid of being vulnerable, so we do not ask for help, and we do not admit when we truly need help.

All these fears coalesce into a mess of restlessness and distrust that leaves us looking like Gollum from *The Lord of the Rings*—hunched over, skittish, alone, clutching whatever power we have, and believing everyone we meet is trying to steal our power from us.

THE LIE REPEATED IN THE BIBLE

THE TOWER OF BABEL

As God's people gather on the plain of Shinar in Genesis 11, they say, "Come, let us build ourselves a city and a tower with its top in the heavens, and let us make a name for ourselves, lest we be dispersed over the face of the whole earth" (v. 4). These people want to leave a legacy. They want to make a name for themselves. They want to seize control of their own destinies and put down as deep of roots as they can by building as high of a tower as they can. They want to be the people with the tower so that everyone will know them. They want this tower to be their focal point of unity.

Such temptation to power and glory can come only from Satan. Satan is always encouraging us toward more fame, to finding more of our identity in actions and accomplishments, to bigger and better. Satan is always trying to get us to attach our identity and unity to anything other than God.

> *Such temptation to power and glory can come only from Satan.*

Life will be better, Satan lies, if you protect yourselves from being scattered, if you seize more control and focus all your attention on this building project.

Of course, God comes down and confuses the language of the people and causes the very thing they fear—their scattering to the ends of the earth, their division, their weakening and loss of control. There is no name made for them, for they are given myriad names and are not even able to understand what the others are called. Their legacy is one of arrogant foolishness.

In seeking to seize a better life, the people of Babel experience one of the fruits of Satan's lies: division.

ABRAM, SARAI, AND HAGAR

God promises Abram that his offspring will be as numerous as the stars in the sky. But after waiting for several years, Abram and Sarai come to the conclusion that they need to do something in order for this promise to take place. Perhaps they start by thinking that the promise was only made to Abram, not to the both of them, so perhaps the promise could be fulfilled if Abram became a father with someone other than his wife. Sarai suggests Hagar, her servant. Abram takes Sarai's suggestion, and Hagar has a son, Ishmael. But God did not need Abram and Sarai to take matters into their own hands. God would fulfill His promise of a child in His own time. Isaac is born, the child of the promise, twenty-five years after the promise is made.

In taking matters into their own hands, seizing control of the situation, and seeking to guide the promise to their own liking, Abram and Sarai abuse Hagar. Hagar has no say in being given to Abram. Sarai mistreats Hagar to the extent that Hagar runs away, terrified. Hagar returns at the urging of the angel of the Lord and stays for several years. But then, sometime after Isaac is born, the renamed Abraham and Sarah send Hagar and Ishmael away. Ishmael nearly dies in the wilderness, but he and Hagar are saved by the angel of the Lord.

Eventually the tables will turn, as Isaac's grandson Joseph will be sold to Ishmael's descendants as a slave and brought down to Egypt, Hagar's homeland. And God will find a way to bring about good in the midst of so much evil. Despite His people constantly seeking to seize control away from Him, God will guide things for eventual good.

HEROD'S SLAUGHTER OF THE INNOCENTS

One of the most disturbing stories in the Scriptures is that of King Herod slaughtering children in the region of Bethlehem. Within a couple of years of Jesus being born, Magi (also known as Wise Men) had come from the East, seeking the King of the Jews. They show up in Jerusalem, and Herod the Great invites them in so he can learn more about this new king. Herod pretends that he wants to go and worship the child king as well and tells the Magi to return to him and inform him of the child's whereabouts. But Herod just wants to kill the child and remove any threat to his throne. God warns the Magi not to return to Herod, and God likewise warns Joseph so that he, Mary, and Jesus flee to Egypt.

Tragically, Herod's lust for power cannot keep him from seeking to assassinate a child. His belief in Satan's lie to seize more control drives him to kill a child. That is horrifying enough, but when Herod can't find said child king, he chooses to kill every male child in the region of Bethlehem. "Collateral damage" was not in Herod's vocabulary.

Satan's lie to Herod that he must seize control to keep his throne and eliminate any possible challengers leads to death—the death of infants. These unknown martyrs from unknown families haunt the pages of the Scriptures with a warning to us all; the lust for power leads to a soul so disfigured it cannot recognize right from wrong, good from evil.

How sad and horrifying it is that, in the end, Adam and Eve's eating from the tree of the knowledge of good and evil can lead to such complete and willful ignorance of good and evil.

> *The lust for power leads to a soul so disfigured it cannot recognize right from wrong, good from evil.*

THE LIE REPEATED IN OUR WORLD

Using our power and control is something we do automatically. Sometimes this is necessary and warranted. When we are hungry, we find something to eat. When we are tired, we try to get some rest or find a cup of coffee. When we want to see New Zealand, we make plans to visit. We all have vocations and responsibilities. These are all good and proper.

The problem of control comes when we lose sight of the reality that God is the Creator of all things and we are His stewards. As stewards, we are given responsibility over God's good gifts, but we do not own them. God does.

Likewise, Adam and Eve are exiled from the Garden of Eden at least in part because they are bad tenants and poor stewards. They have reached out and taken from the one tree they were forbidden to eat from as if they owned it. But they did not and do not own it. God does. They did not own Eden or the trees or animals. God owns Eden. God owns the trees and animals and all creation.

We are not able to usurp the authority of God. When Satan lies to us and tells us that life will be better if we seize more control, he is trying to persuade us to usurp God's authority for our own, to abdicate our role as stewards and go for the top job: being God.

Through this lie, Satan attempts to form us to be more like him, to be made in his image: power hungry, arrogant, and proud.

We do not have to look very hard to see people seizing control in our world today. Major power moves make news headlines. Any example of genocide comes from people believing this lie. The political world is filled with fights over power. And no matter what nation you live in or political affiliations you hold, I think all of us believe to some extent that if our preferred political party had more control and less opposition, the world would be better. Satan wants us to think this and, moreover, to do whatever is necessary to make it occur. Whether it is digging up dirt on opponents to embarrass them, tampering with elections, or leading an outright coup d'état, Satan tells us nothing should get in the way of claiming power. Lies, threats, bribes, and murder are all fair game. The ends justify the means, Satan says. But Satan is a liar. After all, what is his eventual end? To have his head crushed and be banished from all of God's goodness.

Yet this lie is not told merely to those who hold power on a grand scale. This lie is lived out in small ways in our homes every day. How often have you sat around complaining about something that you could obviously fix if you had more control? You would have written a better ending to that book. You would have installed the TV perfectly centered and level (and in much less time). You would have caught that touchdown pass. You would never have dried out the chicken if you were cooking.

We must discern whether our acts of power—big or small—are faithful stewardship of God's good gifts. It is perfectly good stewardship of the power entrusted to you to make dinner when you are hungry. But if you and a work colleague are in competition for a promotion and you decide to murder your colleague, that is quite obviously unfaithful stewardship of what God has given you.

Most decisions find themselves in between these obvious examples of right and wrong.

Sadly, this lie plays out in the church with regularity, at both local and institutional levels. Imagine what would happen in your congregation if someone rearranged the church kitchen. Imagine what would happen if someone painted the sanctuary a different color without informing anyone else. Imagine what would happen if you closed the school affiliated with your church without warning. Some of us do not have to imagine these things because they have happened to us. Control was seized. The fruit of such actions is often anger, pain, division, and—if Satan can manage it—hatred.

Usually, though, this lie plays out behind the curtain. It happens when people show up to church an hour early so that things can be decorated "the right way." It happens when people are prevented from serving in certain church positions for reasons of petty preference. It happens when an abusive pastor is protected by his congregation and superiors.

Yet the place where Christians find themselves most obviously struggling with this lie, especially in the United States, is in the realm of culture wars. For decades, being a Christian was the norm in the United

States. According to the Pew Research Center, as late as 1991, more than 90 percent of people in the United States identified as Christian. That number decreased to 63 percent by 2022, and all signs point to a continuing downward trend.[10] Furthermore, in today's world, those who identify as Christian apply a wide variety of meaning to the term. Often it is conservative Christians and progressive Christians engaged in a culture war against each other.

Truth is often sacrificed at the altar of power.

While we may hope that the goal of the culture war is truth, truth is often sacrificed at the altar of power. The goal of any war is the seizure of power away from the enemy. In the current American culture wars, there is so much fear that Christians and Christianity will lose cultural influence over the nation and the world that people have abandoned basic decency to gain power. It is as if people believe the future of the church hinges upon having ample power and control to pass on to the next generation.

Dear reader, the future of the church depends on the power and control of only one person: Jesus. Jesus is the past, present, and future of the church. Jesus' authority is the only authority that matters to the church. We are called to follow Him. This need and lust for power and influence over the culture is idolatry. It is not the way of Jesus. Culture wars spur from Satan's lie that you need to seize more power and control.

Believing the lie that we can improve our lives by seizing more control leaves us always hungering for more power and control and never truly satisfied. It leaves us lying in fear every time something does not go our way. It leaves us in broken relationships because we cannot trust

---

10 See "Modeling the Future of Religion in America," Pew Research Center, September 13, 2022, https://www.pewresearch.org/religion/2022/09/13/modeling-the-future-of-religion-in-america/ (accessed May 4, 2024).

anyone. It leaves us looking only to ourselves, distrusting and hating everything and everyone else, including and especially God. The lie that persuades us to seize more control leads us back to believing Lie 1, that we cannot trust God.

This lie takes many forms, including these: I must make my enemies' lives worse for mine to be better. Repaying evil for evil is not only my right but also my responsibility to tip the cosmic scale of justice back to where it should be. And when I seize power, I am somehow different from my power-hungry enemies.

In the end, the seizure of control is a demand that my will be done rather than anyone else's, even God's. This lie flies in the face of what Jesus teaches us to pray: "Thy will be done."

THE TRUTH

The truth is that Jesus calls us quite plainly and obviously to suffer being wronged by those in power. Jesus says, "You have heard that it was said, 'An eye for an eye and a tooth for a tooth.' But I say to you, Do not resist the one who is evil. But if anyone slaps you on the right cheek, turn to him the other also" (Matthew 5:38–39).

Jesus says, "And if anyone would sue you and take your tunic, let him have your cloak as well. And if anyone forces you to go one mile, go with him two miles" (vv. 40–41).

Jesus says, "You have heard that it was said, 'You shall love your neighbor and hate your enemy.' But I say to you, Love your enemies and pray for those who persecute you" (vv. 43–44).

Those who hear Jesus' words and yet justify seeking and seizing power for some greater good simply do not have ears to hear. They choose to listen to the lie rather than the truth.

Jesus calls us to a humility and humbleness that looks weak and meek to the world. And Jesus calls such meekness blessed: "Blessed are the meek, for they shall inherit the earth" (v. 5).

The truth is that all authority in heaven *and on earth* has been given to Jesus, not to us.

Remember the parable of the wedding feast from the previous chapter. Everyone who chooses to exalt themselves by means of seizing a chair they do not deserve will be humbled. Everyone who seizes any sort of power will be humbled. When we seize power and when we buy this lie, we will be humbled, brought low, perhaps even disgraced. Jesus calls us to the lowest place. Jesus calls us to meekness and weakness, promising His strength will shine.

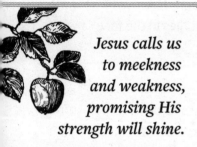

Jesus calls us to meekness and weakness, promising His strength will shine.

GOD'S DESIRED OUTCOME

God's desired outcome is that we become more and more like Jesus. God's desire is that we become more humble, gentle, and meek. We are called to be imitators of God.

As noted earlier, Jesus gives us this counterintuitive blessing: "Blessed are the meek, for they shall inherit the earth" (Matthew 5:5).

Also, Jesus directly invites us to learn this from Him. He says, "Take My yoke upon you, and learn from Me, for I am gentle and lowly in heart, and you will find rest for your souls" (Matthew 11:29).

The word translated as "meek" in Matthew 5:5 is the same word that is translated as "gentle" in Matthew 11:29. A yoke is a farming implement used for a pair of animals, often oxen, horses, or donkeys. The pair of animals works together, harnessed together by the yoke, pulling a plow or a cart. Jesus calls us to be yoked to Him, to be teamed with Him. In so doing, He calls on us to learn from Him. Learn His rhythms and pace, His character and way of acting in the world.

What is Jesus' character? It is typified by gentleness, humbleness, and meekness. Jesus is almighty and all powerful, yet He comes in meekness. He acts in humility. As Paul writes,

> **Have this mind among yourselves, which is yours in Christ Jesus, who, though He was in the form of God, did not count equality with God a thing to be grasped, but emptied Himself, by taking the form of a servant, being born in the likeness of men. And being found in human form, He humbled Himself by becoming obedient to the point of death, even death on a cross.** (Philippians 2:5–8)

God's desired outcome is that we become more and more like Jesus, that we humble ourselves and allow God to be the one who exalts us, just as He exalts Jesus.

Ultimately, we must reckon with the reality that Jesus, with all authority in heaven and on earth, chose to empty Himself of all His power not once but twice. He chose to empty Himself when He became a human being. He became entirely dependent, entrusting His life to two human beings who were no more powerful than you or me. Then Jesus emptied Himself of all His power even further by dying And not just dying, but dying a criminal's death, suffering through the agony of an execution He did not deserve.

Jesus trusted God's will so fully that He went to the cross and died, trusting that God would raise Him from the dead. Jesus had the power to stop this. But when His followers tried to prevent His arrest, He stopped them. When Peter took up a sword in Gethsemane, Jesus told him, "Put your sword back into its place. For all who take the sword will perish by the sword. Do you think that I cannot appeal to My Father, and He will at once send Me more than twelve legions[11] of angels?" (Matthew 26:52–53).

---

11 *Legion* was a Roman military term. In Jesus' time, a legion likely would have consisted of around five thousand soldiers. More than twelve legions of angels meant more than sixty thousand angelic soldiers.

This is the power Jesus holds, yet Jesus did not seize control. Jesus allowed Himself to die.

Jesus did not seize control. Jesus allowed Himself to die.

God's desired outcome is that we become more like Jesus. This means being more sacrificial and less controlling, more of a servant and less of a narcissist, more trusting of Jesus as the one who is in control.

THE LOVE THAT CASTS OUT FEAR

As we have seen, often we seize power and control because we are afraid of being taken advantage of. We are afraid of being vulnerable. We are afraid that there is no one on earth we can trust. The love that casts out this fear is Jesus, the man from heaven who came down to earth out of love for His fallen creation.

Jesus loves you. Jesus saves you from sin, death, and the devil by His death and resurrection. Jesus does this not by seizing power but by laying it down.

Peter writes, "Humble yourselves, therefore, under the mighty hand of God so that at the proper time He may exalt you, casting all your anxieties on Him, because He cares for you" (1 Peter 5:6–7). We sometimes separate these two verses, but consider their impact together. We can humble ourselves because God cares for us. Our anxieties and worries will push us to seize more power and control, but Jesus invites us to cast all those cares and anxieties upon Him. He cares for us. No one can seize power from His hand.

God's love for us is not lacking. God's care for us is not scarce. He knows what we need. Jesus tells us, "Are not five sparrows sold for two pennies? And not one of them is forgotten before God. Why, even the hairs of your head are all numbered. Fear not; you are of more value than many sparrows" (Luke 12:6–7). God's care for birds and flowers is abundantly clear. God, likewise and even more so, cares for you. He will never take advantage of you.

Consider these words from Psalm 18:2: "The LORD is my rock and my fortress and my deliverer, my God, my rock, in whom I take refuge, my shield, and the horn of my salvation, my stronghold."

Sometimes we usurp God's place and try to be our own fortress, our own shield, and our own deliverer. But such roles must be left to the One who can actually accomplish the task, and that is not you or me. That is Jesus only. Our fear of being taken advantage of must be handed over to the Creator, who cannot be taken advantage of by His creation and who will never take advantage of you.

Questions for Reflection

Where do you see this lie appearing in your life?

In what situations have you been most tempted to seize control?

Can you remember a time when you were afraid of being manipulated? What was that like?

Whom can you trust to tell you the truth when you are struggling with this lie?

Can you think of other biblical characters who unhelpfully seized control?

Scripture for Meditation

Psalm 46

2 Samuel 11:1–12:14

John 13:1–20

LIE 5

YOU ARE EXEMPT

(THAT DOESN'T APPLY TO YOU)

I am guessing that as you looked through the table of contents, this lie did not immediately resonate with you. But hear me out through a few simple examples.

A professional athlete once came to speak at my middle school. He told us about the incredibly low probability of becoming a professional athlete. Statistically, chances were that nobody in the room was going to play sports professionally. Twelve-year-old me sat there thinking, "Yeah, but that doesn't apply to me."

Every March, I fill out a bracket for the NCAA men's and women's basketball tournaments. Every year, I dream about being the first person in history to get a perfect bracket. The odds of this are astronomically impossible. I have a better chance of living on Mars, I think. And most years, I get the first game wrong.

When I was growing up, it was a rule in our house that if you were the one to finish a pitcher of juice or lemonade, you had to make another one. I did everything I could to avoid that task. I would drink half of a glass instead of a whole one. I would drink milk instead. On occasion, I would literally walk over to my grandparents' house (they lived on the same farm as us) and drink their juice rather than empty the pitcher from my house.

Perhaps you have done something similar. Perhaps you noticed something was wrong but did not speak up about it, just waited for somebody else to discover it. Maybe you noticed a child's seemingly dirty diaper but cleverly shuffled the child off to someone else for them to discover and change it.

Whether it is the silliest or the most serious thing, we try to wriggle out of things applying to us.

The lengths to which we will go to exempt ourselves are staggering. Whether it is the silliest or the most serious thing, we try to wriggle out of things applying to us.

SATAN IN THE GARDEN

The lie begins as Satan says to Eve, "You will not surely die" (Genesis 3:4). God had told Adam, "You may surely eat of every tree of the garden, but of the tree of the knowledge of good and evil you shall not eat, for in the day that you eat of it you shall surely die" (Genesis 2:16–17). Satan lies to Eve and convinces her that she and Adam are exempt from God's Word, that the threat of death God proclaimed does not apply to them. But Satan lied. Adam and Eve both die.

Satan persuades them that they are exempt from the rule and thereby exempt from the consequence. He does this by pointing out the benefit (if you can call it that) of eating the forbidden fruit: "Your eyes will be opened, and you will be like God" (Genesis 3:5). Follow the logic here: If Adam and Eve will be like God, then how could death be a possibility? Death does not apply to God, so it makes sense that death would not apply to those who are like God. Satan is not only saying they are exempt from death but also arguing that eating this forbidden fruit is the very way in which to gain exemption from death. They will be like God.

What Adam and Eve fail to recognize is that God is already protecting them from death. They are exempt from death, but by their disobedience, they receive exactly what God had spoken. Having tasted from the tree of the knowledge of good and evil, they are now forbidden from tasting the tree of life. Hence, they will taste death.

The temptation to exempt ourselves is rooted in a desire for significance. We want to know that we matter, that our lives have purpose and meaning. If our lives look too much like the rest of the world, that can make us uncomfortable, and we attempt to stand out in some fashion to prove that we have significance. One way to stand out is to exempt ourselves. We might exempt ourselves from the rules. We might exempt ourselves from good news. We might exempt ourselves from bad news.

SATAN IN THE WILDERNESS

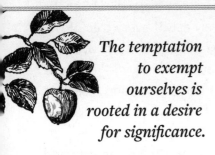

The temptation to exempt ourselves is rooted in a desire for significance.

Satan uses this lie against Jesus on two occasions. Both times, Satan seeks to persuade Jesus to exempt Himself from being human. First, Satan says, "If You are the Son of God, command these stones to become loaves of bread" (Matthew 4:3). In effect, Satan is trying to convince Jesus that, as the Son of God, He ought to be exempt from any of the inconveniences that humans must deal with. Hunger should be meaningless to Jesus. He should be exempt from it. He should (pairing with the previous lie) seize more control and exempt Himself from hunger.

Second, Satan attempts to persuade Jesus of His exemption from humanity: "If You are the Son of God, throw Yourself down, for it is written, 'He will command His angels concerning you,' and 'On their hands they will bear you up, lest you strike your foot against a stone'" (v. 6).

In effect, Satan is saying, "Come on, Jesus, if You are the Son of God, You will be exempt from the consequences of other human beings. Surely gravity is meaningless to one who has angels at His command."

In this encounter with Jesus, Satan is putting forward a complicated combination of accusation and temptation that seeks to distance Jesus from both His divinity and His humanity. If Jesus is truly the Son of God, as the Father says at Jesus' Baptism, then Jesus need not continue the charade of masking Himself in human frailty and weakness. Simultaneously, Satan's words in this scene cast doubt on God's Word that Jesus is God's beloved Son: "If You are the Son of God . . ." (v. 3). Satan wants Jesus to showcase His divinity or His humanity.

Satan wants Jesus to choose one and abandon the other. "If You are the Son of God . . . show it."

Satan wants to distance Jesus either from His heavenly Father or from humanity. Either one will do. If Jesus turns stones into bread for Himself to eat, He distances Himself from humanity. In Jesus' answer to Satan, Jesus identifies with humanity, saying that this Scripture applies to Him as a human being: "Man shall not live by bread alone, but by every word that comes from the mouth of God" (v. 4).

In the temptation accounts, Satan wants Jesus to show His divinity through self-serving power. What is so interesting to me is that Jesus does begin to show His power almost immediately after this scene. But He does not do so to serve Himself; instead, He shows His power through healing, serving others, and casting out Satan's forces. Jesus does not leave Satan in the dark about who He truly is. Jesus shows Satan and the whole world by casting out demons, walking on the sea, and raising the dead.

SATAN IN THE HEAVENLY COUNCIL

In the opening chapters of the book of Job, we see a strange scene where Satan stands in God's presence, in the heavenly council. God invites Satan to consider His servant Job. God says of Job, "There is none like him on the earth, a blameless and upright man, who fears God and turns away from evil" (Job 1:8). Satan accuses Job of being blameless and upright only because God has exempted Job from suffering. God has put a hedge of protection around Job, exempting Job from Satan's usual ability to wreak havoc in the life of God's people. "Does Job fear God for no reason?" Satan asks (v. 9). To Satan, Job's fear of the Lord and his blameless and upright life are cheap because God has protected Job from life's problems. Satan wants to wreck Job's life, ruin his wealth, murder his children, and disfigure him with as much pain as possible. Which is exactly what happens.

In this case, Satan lies even to God from the midst of the heavenly council. No one is exempt from being lied to by Satan. It is his character, his native language. Remember, being lied to is not a sin. Trusting Satan's lies and acting according to them is where we all make mistakes.

SATAN'S DESIRED OUTCOME

On the surface, Satan wants this lie to produce in us a disregard for consequences. When we believe we are exempt from consequences, we tend to act badly, to sin, to disobey.

But deeper than that, behind the lie that we are exempt is the truth that we are different from others, that we are unique. Satan uses our uniqueness to direct us toward shame or pride. The lie that we are exempt may push us toward inferiority. Satan might tell you that you are flawed differently than others, that you are worse than, less interesting, and less talented. He pushes us to isolate and exempt ourselves from what is good, true, and beautiful. But at the same time, Satan uses this lie to make us feel superior to everyone. Satan might tell you that you are better than others, more interesting, more talented, that you are deeper. Such superiority leads us to exempt ourselves from anything mundane that does not make us the center of the universe.

> *Satan uses our uniqueness to direct us toward shame or pride.*

However we are most prone to isolate ourselves, Satan will push us toward such exemptions. If we are prone to arrogance, Satan will push us toward superiority. If we are prone to shame, Satan will push us toward inferiority.

Consider the outcome if we exempt ourselves from some of these truths of good news:

Jesus loves you. If you exempt yourself from this truth, you honestly believe Jesus loves everybody else in the world, just not you. Satan tries to persuade each of us that there is something about us that is different, something that is off and askew that prevents Jesus' love from reaching us. (More on this in Lie 10.)

You are forgiven. If you exempt yourself from this truth, you disbelieve the power of Jesus' death and resurrection. You allow sin to be more powerful than Jesus and His saving actions.

Love your neighbor as yourself. If you exempt yourself from this truth, you will expect everyone else to keep on treating others with kindness and love, but you will leave space for yourself to continue hating others. Loving one's neighbor becomes transactionally based in reciprocity, in how it benefits you, in what you can get out of it.

Satan's desired outcome with this lie is to lead us into thinking we are at the extremes of being better or worse than everyone else in the world. If we head toward "worse than all others," Satan will tell more lies that lead us toward the outcome of despair (see Lies 7, 9, and 10). If we head toward "better than all others," Satan will tell more lies that lead us toward the outcome of arrogance and superiority (see Lies 3 and 4).

THE FEAR BEHIND THE LIE

The fear behind the lie of being exempt is that of being without significance or meaning. It is such a crooked lie. Satan often starts by lying with the fear itself: "You don't matter. You are meaningless. Your life is pointless." Then Satan offers a contrasting solution out of the other side of his mouth: "But you are different. You are unique. You are unlike anyone else in the world." Discombobulated, afraid, and seeking meaning in our uniqueness, we are primed for the main lie to arrive: "Exclude yourself. Don't let what applies to everyone else apply to you. How else will you know you have meaning unless you stand out as different?"

Satan wants our fear of insignificance to drive us toward seeking significance apart from others and especially apart from Jesus.

What is devastating about this is that you *are* unique. You are a one-of-a-kind, treasured masterpiece. But as Satan pushes you toward uniqueness, he begins to interchange uniqueness for exemption. The uniqueness that each of us has is a wonderful gift, but it is not a gift to be cherished alone. Our uniqueness is meant to bless the Body of Christ, the community of God's people. Satan wants us to find all our meaning and identity apart from Jesus and His people. Satan twists the good gift of our uniqueness into a paradox of superiority and inferiority that pushes us away from others and away from Jesus.

> *The uniqueness that each of us has is a wonderful gift, but it is not a gift to be cherished alone.*

Imagine a large puzzle with thousands of pieces. Each piece is unique. No two pieces are interchangeable. Some pieces look similar. There are six basic shapes most pieces take. But in nearly every puzzle, a few pieces do not fit the typical pattern. As you build a puzzle, you do not try to fit those atypical pieces into typical spots. You know they will not fit. Imagine if a puzzle piece had emotions. Imagine how left out it would begin to feel after seeing every piece in the box being tried to fit before it. Satan would push such a puzzle piece toward exemption by inferiority: "Look around. You look nothing like these other pieces. You clearly don't belong here. In fact, I've never seen a piece like you. Maybe you don't belong to any puzzle. You must be a mistake, a glitch. Maybe you're just a piece of cardboard garbage."

Or perhaps Satan would push such a piece toward exemption by superiority. "Look at all these other pieces. They're all virtually the same. But not you. You are different. Look at the combination of jagged and smooth lines on you. You are better than all of these. So much better, why even deign to be a part of this boring puzzle?"

As human beings, we are far more varied than puzzle pieces and far more important. Satan knows we are afraid of insignificance and that we crave to know that we matter to God and to others. Satan uses our fear to distance us from God and others. Exempting ourselves always creates distance and pushes us toward the final two lies of the book, "You are alone" and "You are too flawed to be forgiven."

THE LIE REPEATED IN THE BIBLE

ANANIAS AND SAPPHIRA

In the early chapters of the book of Acts, the apostles witness boldly to the resurrection of Jesus, and a community of believers forms. These believers live a communal lifestyle. Luke, the author of Acts, writes the following:

> Now the full number of those who believed were of one heart and soul, and no one said that any of the things that belonged to him was his own, but they had everything in common. And with great power the apostles were giving their testimony to the resurrection of the Lord Jesus, and great grace was upon them all. There was not a needy person among them, for as many as were owners of lands or houses sold them and brought the proceeds of what was sold and laid it at the apostles' feet, and it was distributed to each as any had need. (Acts 4:32–35)

It does not take long for someone to take advantage of this movement of charity. A couple named Ananias and Sapphira sell a piece of property. They want to keep some of the profits for themselves, but they also want everyone to think that they had charitably given the whole value of the property. So they conspire together to lie to the apostles and the church regarding the property's selling price.

The Holy Spirit reveals the deception to Peter, and Peter confronts Ananias as soon as the gift is given, saying, "Ananias, why has Satan filled your heart to lie to the Holy Spirit and to keep back for yourself part of the proceeds of the land? While it remained unsold, did it not remain your own? And after it was sold, was it not at your disposal? Why is it that you have contrived this deed in your heart? You have not lied to man but to God" (Acts 5:3–4). Ananias drops dead. His wife, Sapphira, comes in a bit later and likewise lies, and she falls dead too.

The lie that Satan fills their hearts with is multifaceted. Yes, they believe they need and deserve more than others. Yes, they seize more power by holding onto more money. Yes, they believe they should cover up the lie as well (we will talk about that in the next chapter). But the main facet to the lie is that Ananias and Sapphira believe they are exempt from the community's standards, that they can act differently than others yet take credit for being the same.

As Peter tells Ananias, it would have been completely fine if they had chosen not to sell the land. It would have been fine if they had chosen to give only a portion of the sale or none. The problem is the deception, saying they were giving the full amount when they were giving only a portion.

Ananias and Sapphira believe the truth does not apply to them, that they are exempt from it. They pay with their very lives.

NO LONGER KING SAUL

God's people demand a king. God gives them Saul. For a while, things are well with Saul as king of Israel. But eventually, Saul disobeys the Lord, and God tears the kingdom away from him. Saul still clings to power. He still maintains the throne for a time after his rejection, but God has chosen David to serve as king. What David does prospers. What Saul does withers.

Saul hears the Word of the Lord proclaimed through the prophet Samuel: "Because you have rejected the word of the Lord, He has also rejected you from being king" (1 Samuel 15:23). Even in this rejection,

Saul clings to power. Saul grabs at Samuel's robe as he goes to leave, and it tears. Samuel then tells Saul, "The LORD has torn the kingdom of Israel from you this day and has given it to a neighbor of yours, who is better than you" (v. 28).

Saul begins losing his grip on the kingdom. And worse, Saul loses access to the Word of the Lord. Immediately after this, Saul and Samuel go their separate ways. They do not see each other again, even though Samuel grieves over Saul (see vv. 34–35).

Before and after Samuel's death, Saul desperately seeks to hear from the Lord, but nothing works. When Saul inquires of the Lord, he receives no answer, "either by dreams, or by Urim, or by prophets" (28:6). So Saul resorts to a means he knows is wrong, to something he himself has forbidden in Israel: a medium. Saul seeks out a person who can communicate with the dead. Saul requests the medium bring up Samuel from the dead so that Saul can talk to him. It is a very strange scene, but what Samuel says to Saul is heartbreaking: "Why then do you ask me, since the LORD has turned from you and become your enemy? The LORD has done to you as He spoke by me, for the LORD has torn the kingdom out of your hand and given it to your neighbor, David" (vv. 16–17).

Saul exempts himself from his own rule in order to hear from Samuel and hear from the Lord. He embraces the use of something he knows God is against in order to hear from the Lord. In his distress, Saul tragically listens to the lie that he is exempt. He believes the lie that he can do whatever he needs to do in order to hear from the Lord, even when the means is forbidden by the Lord.

Saul says that the Lord will no longer speak to him. Yet that is not the problem. The problem is that the Lord *did* speak, and Saul did not listen. Saul was

> *Saul exempted himself from that Word of the Lord and kept looking for a different word.*

rejected from being king. Saul exempted himself from that Word of the Lord and kept looking for a different word. But there was no other word for him to hear. God was merely doing what He had promised years before because of Saul's disobedience. And now, with one more act of disobedience, Saul learns the last thing he wanted to hear: that his death will be the following day (vv. 18–19).

Saul exempts himself from his own rule, from God's rule, and from God's very clear prophetic word that Saul's kingship is over. His desperation and presumption bring him to a panicked, fearful life in which he succumbs to Satan's lies in perpetuity. Saul seeks more control. He exempts himself. And in the end, he shows his distrust of God and His Word.

THE PRODIGAL SON

In Luke 15:11–32, Jesus tells a story about a father and his two sons. The younger son exempts himself from the family, demanding his share of the inheritance. The normal rule in that culture was that any inheritance would be given only on the death of the father. But the younger son exempts himself from the rules and wants his share right now. The father bizarrely agrees to this. The younger son goes off to a faraway land and spends all his inheritance. Then a famine hits, and nobody will take care of him. When he finally realizes that he can go home and be taken care of, even if it is merely as a servant, he goes back to his father's house. Then something happens that he does not anticipate—he is welcomed home as a son. Though he had exempted himself from the family, he is given back his place as a son, a status he absolutely does not deserve.

His older brother hears what has happened and is furious. What does he do? He exempts himself from celebrating his prodigal brother's return. He exempts himself from the family. When his father comes out to invite him into the celebration, the older son shares something so sad. He tells his father, "Look, these many years I have served you, and I never disobeyed your command, yet you never gave me a young goat, that I might celebrate with my friends" (Luke 15:29). The older son is struggling with Lie 2, that his value is based on his performance. He thinks he needs to earn his father's favor. He thinks his younger brother needs to earn his father's favor. The older son is disgusted that his own family would reward such wretched behavior, and he does not want to celebrate with a family that acts like that.

I can hear the older son yelling out in frustration at his father, "What about me, Dad?"

His father's words show something that perhaps the older son had never realized: "Son, you are always with me, and all that is mine is yours" (v. 31). The older son does not need permission to celebrate with his friends. He can do that any time he likes. He does not need permission to kill a young goat or even the fattened calf. Those things already belong to him. In exempting himself from the celebration, the older son merely exempts himself from what is good.

Both sons seem to fear they are insignificant. The younger thinks he can find significance on his own with a pile of money. He is wrong. The older thinks he can find significance by his performance as a dutiful son. He is wrong. Both sons have significance in this: they belong to the family, and they are loved by their father.

THE LIE REPEATED IN OUR WORLD

The biblical examples above are tragic life-and-death situations. In our day-to-day lives, our exemptions are harder to see because we have come to accept them as normal.

Often our self-exemption from particular rules or sins involves us subconsciously asking, "How much can I get away with?"

> *Our exemptions are harder to see because we have come to accept them as normal.*

Speeding is a good example. What is your threshold for testing what you can get away with regarding speeding? Five miles per hour over the speed limit? Ten? More?

If you play golf, how honest are you about your score? How many foot wedges and mulligans are needed for you to get the score you want?

Perhaps we expect our coworkers to show up to work on time every day, but we allow ourselves whatever wiggle room we need if we are not on time.

This lie stretches from exempting ourselves from rules to exempting ourselves from bad news and good news.

Have you ever thought, "Yeah, but that will never happen to me." We do this with illnesses. Around 40 percent of the population will get cancer at some point in their lives. Yet how many of us have ever considered the truth of those numbers? How many of us have quietly assumed we will be exempted from the possibility of cancer? How many people have assumed that right up until the diagnosis?

We do the same thing with divorce. Somewhere between one-third and one-half of all marriages end in divorce. How many of us got married thinking, "Yeah, but that will never happen to us"?

When we exempt ourselves from such potential realities, we are less likely to properly care for these things. If I believe I will never get skin cancer, then I am less likely to wear sunscreen. If I believe my marriage is exempt from divorce statistics, then I am less likely to work on my relationship with my spouse.

While exemption from the rules and bad news is troubling, exemption from good news is far more dangerous. This often happens when we are in a bleak place mentally, emotionally, or spiritually. In such instances, we will begin to expect the worst. When someone tells us we did a good job, we will not believe them. We will deflect and distrust the compliment. When somebody shows us love, we will question it, thinking their actions are a ploy to get something out of us. We will feel patronized and manipulated. We will assume the worst of every-thing and everyone, even God.

In doing this, we inevitably isolate ourselves not only from good news but also from every positive relationship we have. This results in us becoming divided from others and thinking we are superior or inferior to them. Soon, Satan will lead us toward believing that we are exempt from the love, care, and compassion others are trying to show us. And then Satan leads us straight toward Lies 9 and 10, that we are alone and too flawed to be forgiven.

THE TRUTH

The truth is that we are not exempt from God's rules. We are not exempt from the bad news that life is full of problems and suffering. We are not exempt from the good news that Jesus loves us, that He died and rose for our forgiveness and eternal life.

But also, the truth is that you are unique. God made you to be you. Nobody else in the entire world is exactly like you. Your contribution to the world, the church, and your family will be different than anyone else's contribution.

The truth is that your uniqueness stands together with the common-alities you hold with other people. You are unique, and you are part of a community at the same time. Your commonalities do not make you insignificant. Neither does your significance derive from your unique-ness. But both your uniqueness and your commonalities with others are gifts from the same source: Jesus. Your significance comes from Him. Your identity derives from Him.

In the inception of this lie, Satan tries to trick Eve into thinking death could not possibly be an outcome of eating the fruit. Death does not apply to God, so how could eating this fruit and being

You are unique, and you are part of a community at the same time.

like God mean death for Adam and Eve? When Jesus comes into our world, He saves Adam and Eve and us by allowing death to apply to Him. By not exempting Himself from death, Jesus saves those who tried to exempt themselves from it.

GOD'S DESIRED OUTCOME

God's desired outcome (as ever) is the opposite of Satan's. God desires that we recognize that rules, bad news, and good news all apply to us. God does not want us to abandon our uniqueness and blend in with others, nor does God desire that we abandon our commonalities and distance ourselves from others. God desires that we live as the unique creatures He has made us to be in the communities He has placed us in. God desires that we see our uniqueness as a gift, given by the Holy Spirit. Through our uniqueness, we are called to love our neighbors in our unique way. God wants us to see with abundant clarity that we belong with Him. We fit. We are of infinite significance to Him. He sees us for who we truly are, knows us better than we know ourselves, and loves us more than we could ever ask or imagine.

THE LOVE THAT CASTS OUT FEAR

With this amazing love that exceeds our wildest expectations, God longs to cast out our fears of insignificance. He is willing to go to whatever length or height or depth to chase us down, to remind us that nothing can separate us from His love. He is even willing to lay down His life so that we might live eternally with Him. That is how much Jesus longs to spend eternity with you. He dies and conquers death to make it happen.

Consider the love the father shows in the prodigal-son story. The younger son has wished his father dead, and still the father races out to meet his beloved son and welcomes him home with open arms, rich clothing, and a feast of celebration. The older son has exempted himself from the celebration, but his father leaves the celebration in order to retrieve him. The father chases after his son, pleads with him, and reminds him that he belongs in this family.

Both sons fear they have lost their significance and place in the family. Their father chases both down in unwavering, steadfast love and bestows significance and meaning on them by his very own love.

This is what Jesus does for us. He comes down to find us when we are lost or angry or ashamed or feeling like we do not belong. He finds us and gifts us with significance by making us a part of His family. Then He chases after us again and again and again to remind us that we are His family and that nothing can separate us from His love.

Questions for Reflection

Where do you see this lie appearing in your life?

In what situations do you find yourself most likely to exempt yourself from God's Word?

Can you remember a time when you were afraid that your life was not significant? What was that like?

Whom can you trust to tell you the truth when you are struggling with this lie?

Can you think of other biblical characters who exempted themselves from God's Word?

Scripture for Meditation

Matthew 28:16–20

Romans 13:1–7

Titus 3:1–7

LIE 6

YOU SHOULD
COVER UP
YOUR SINS

When I was a kid, my older brother and I were playing baseball in the house (a thing we, of course, were not supposed to do). At one point, the baseball became lodged in a closet door, making a fantastic, baseball-shaped hole. We knew we were breaking the rules. Now the evidence was there against us as plain as day on a door that we all walked past fifty times a day. So what did we do? We drew a quick picture and taped it over the hole in the door. This was not the sort of thing either of us regularly did. It was quite conspicuous. The picture was like a highlighter, pointing my mom right to the scene of the crime and the evidence beneath.

What have you tried to cover up?

SATAN IN THE GARDEN

When Satan succeeds in tempting Adam and Eve into sin in Genesis 3, the first thing they realize is that they are naked. They were naked prior to the fall and unashamed. But now, the fall into sin has caused them to view themselves differently. They feel exposed. They feel unfit to stand naked anymore, even before each other. So they put fig leaves together and cover themselves. They cover the result of their sinful actions.

Then, as they hear God walking in the garden, they hide. They are afraid to be seen in their fallen state. But God comes looking for them and asks, "Where are you?" (Genesis 3:9). Adam answers God's summons and says, "I heard the sound of You in the garden, and I was afraid, because I was naked, and I hid myself" (v. 10). God's reply comes with more questions: "Who told you that you were naked? Have you eaten of the tree of which I commanded you not to eat?" (v. 11).

Then Adam tries to cover up what he did in a different way. He blames Eve. Adam says, "The woman whom You gave to be with me, she gave me fruit of the tree, and I ate" (v. 12). Adam shifts his responsibility onto Eve. She is the one who gave him the fruit.

Adam also covers his disobedience in a more daring way: he blames God. God gave Adam the woman. The woman gave Adam the fruit. Adam avoids his responsibility and abdicates his accountability. He defends himself, not Eve. He defends himself, not God. He tries to squirm out of being at fault by covering his sin from as many angles as possible.

Adam tries to cover up this first sin four times: with fig leaves, by hiding, by blaming Eve, and by blaming God. This reaction, this impulse of covering our sin, still happens. When we try to sort out our sin on our own, our only choice is to try to hide it. We bury our sin away in the deepest, darkest closets of our soul. Or we hide the sin by overlaying it with a coating of sugar so thick that we convince ourselves the sin is somehow palatable.

> *When we try to sort out our sin on our own, our only choice is to try to hide it.*

SATAN'S DESIRED OUTCOME

When people cover up their sin, when people hide their mistakes, the problems and consequences of their sin do not magically go away. Sin festers. Sin grows. If we pretend like sin is not there, if we hide it, things will only become worse and worse.

Imagine a child who wets the bed but is too ashamed to admit it to their parents. So, they simply make their bed, perhaps with an extra blanket or two, and pretend like it didn't happen. The extra blankets won't remove reality. The smell will only gain potency. It may take a day or two, but the truth will come out. It is no sin to wet the bed. It is no sin to feel embarrassed. But covering up something will not make it go away.

Satan knows the power of sin. Satan knows that hiding sin makes it blossom and flourish. Satan knows that when sin is confessed and repented of, it is forgiven. He does not want that. Satan's desire is to keep people trapped and hidden in any and every sin he can so that the effects of those sins will keep festering and multiplying. Like mold on a slice of bread spreads through the whole loaf, Satan's desired outcome is for hidden sin to spread and infect our whole lives.

This lie is particularly useful to Satan because he knows the only way to keep sin covered in secrecy is to lie. If we believe the lie that we need to hide sin, we will lie and lie and lie in order to keep the sin hidden. Here Satan achieves another desired outcome: we become more and more like Satan, the father of lies. This is why Satan glories in this particular lie; it makes God's people less like God and more like Satan. This lie builds its own scaffolding of lies that all keep pulling people further and further away from Jesus, which is Satan's ultimate goal. Satan wants us to forget that we are made in God's image. He wants us to forget that our sin is forgiven in Jesus.

When I was in the third grade, sometime in the fall, one of our class projects involved glitter. Each student was given a plastic container of glitter. When it was time to turn in the glitter containers at the end of the week, one was missing. The teacher couldn't figure it out. Well, it was mine. I had accidentally broken it. In a desire to hide this, I had shoved it into the depths of my desk, where no one would see it. Months later, in the final days of the school year, we were cleaning out our desks. I pulled out my glitter container and threw it away along with a bunch of other trash so that it would be buried and unseen, and the mystery of the missing glitter container continued and was forgotten.

Part of the reason Satan loves this lie is because sometimes we humans *seem* to succeed at keeping things hidden. That ability to keep something hidden and secret, particularly something as silly as a broken glitter container, convinces us that we can successfully hide other things.

But long after everyone else has forgotten about the glitter containers and how one was missing, I remember. I remember that I lied to my teacher about it. I remember that I pretended not to know the truth. The lie kept doing its work even though I had gotten away with it.

Even when we think such hidden-ness has been successful, Satan loves to bring those instances of shame back to the forefront of our minds and make us feel like garbage. We could be having a perfectly good day with smiles and laughter and tacos, when out of nowhere we are abruptly reminded of that time in the high school cafeteria when we cruelly made fun of a friend and ruined a relationship. We could be having a perfectly normal day at work when we are suddenly reminded of a time we lost our temper and screamed at the people we love most in this world and made them feel terrified of us. We could be in bed just about to fall asleep when a stray thought of something shameful from years past leaps back to the surface of our minds and frightens us awake.

> *Satan loves to bring those instances of shame back to the forefront of our minds and make us feel like garbage.*

Satan will conjure up both the darkest and weakest moments of our lives whenever he can to keep us from love, joy, peace, and anything else associated with the Holy Spirit.

THE FEAR BEHIND THE LIE

On the surface, this lie often looks like a fear of conflict. Adam hides from God in hopes of avoiding the conflict and confrontation with God that he knows is coming. But if you ask anyone who routinely avoids conflict (*raises hand*), they will likely tell you that conflict is not the true fear that leads them to hide. Conflict is dangerous because it raises uncertainty about the relationship. Conflict introduces a deeper fear—the fear of being separated or abandoned, of damaging a relationship beyond repair.

When Adam falls into sin and seeks to cover it up, he admits that he is afraid. He has plenty of reasons for fear. He is naked and exposed. He knows he has messed up. The world around him has changed so completely and so quickly. Perhaps Adam is afraid that his relationship with God is over, and he does not want to hear that bad news.

Here Satan preys on the illogical and irrational hypotheticals of our fear. Adam hides from God. Adam seeks to exile himself from his relationship with God before God can abandon him. Sometimes the fear of the other person severing a relationship prompts someone to preemptively end it themselves. Diabolically, fear pushes us to cause the thing we fear to happen. When we fear that a relationship is damaged, we may avoid learning whether our fears are true. Our actions of avoidance and covering, motivated by fear, may amplify and accelerate the damage.

Other fears lurk in the background of this lie: The fear of being shamed and made to feel worthless. The fear of being invaded and overwhelmed by other people's reactions. The fear that conflict will arise if people ever find out what we have done or has been done to us. The fear of relationships being damaged and ended. Secrecy, we think, will protect us from all these fears. And it may, at least for a time. But secrets, especially secrets of sin, do not sit still. They linger restlessly, thanks to Satan, who uses this lie to torment us with many other lies: "You are broken beyond repair. You couldn't even admit to accidentally breaking a coffee mug." "You are perfectly fine. You are exempt from confessing to petty nonsense like this. It's beneath you, and so are the people telling you to confess." "Wow. You cannot even stand up for yourself. You are too weak and irrelevant to matter to God. Why would He want you in His kingdom?"

Secrets, especially secrets of sin, do not sit still.

THE LIE REPEATED IN THE BIBLE

CAIN AND ABEL

After Adam and Eve fall into sin and are exiled from the Garden of Eden, God eventually blesses them with a family. In time, Eve gives birth to two sons, Cain and Abel. As they grow up, Cain learns to be a gardener, a keeper of the ground. Abel learns to be a shepherd, a keeper of sheep. One day as they bring their sacrifices to God, God approves of Abel's sacrifice but disregards Cain's sacrifice. God's reasoning is not explained. Abel brings "the firstborn of his flock and of their fat portions" (Genesis 4:4). This sounds (at least for those of us who have read ahead in the biblical story) like Abel is bringing the absolute best offering he can. Cain's offering is described much more simply—"an offering of the fruit of the ground" (v. 3). It could be that Cain did not bring the choicest selection of his produce and grain. Abel was clearly thoughtful in how he was going to honor God. Perhaps Cain was less thoughtful in his offering. The Lord says to Cain, "Why are you angry, and why has your face fallen? If you do well, will you not be accepted? And if you do not do well, sin is crouching at the door. Its desire is contrary to you, but you must rule over it" (vv. 6–7). It seems from God's answer that Cain did not "do well" with his offering. We are not told what the problem is, but Cain is about to escalate the problem so that we forget all about his disregarded offering.

Cain takes Abel out into a field and murders him. Immediately after this occurs, God says to Cain, "Where is Abel your brother?"

Cain replies, "I do not know; am I my brother's keeper?" (v. 9).

Satan incites Cain three times. Satan incites Cain to be downcast and angry. Satan incites Cain to murder Abel. And Satan lurks in the background, telling Cain, "You must cover up your sin." Cain has the audacity, the nerve, to lie to God's face: "I do not know." Abel's lifeless body lies in the field where Cain left it. Abel's blood seeps into

117

the cursed ground that Cain has gardened and tended. And Cain lies to cover up what he has done.

"I don't know" is one of the easiest lies to tell. When we break something accidentally, for some reason, it is much easier to say, "I don't know how it broke," than the truth, "I was clumsy and I dropped it and it broke." It is easier to throw the thing away and hide it from sight and pretend like you have no idea what happened to it.

JOSEPH'S BROTHERS

In Genesis 37, most of Jacob's sons are off taking care of the flock many miles from home. Jacob sends his favorite son, Joseph, to see how they are doing. Joseph is hated by his brothers. Jacob openly prefers Joseph, showering him with a lavish gift of a one-of-a-kind robe. Joseph does not help matters by relaying how, in his dreams, his brothers (and even his mother and father) will one day bow down to him.

Joseph goes to find his brothers, but they decide to dispose of this dreamer. They strip Joseph of his fancy robe, throw him into a dry cistern, and argue about whether to kill him. Then along comes opportunity. A group of Ishmaelite traders rides past on their way down to Egypt. The brothers sell Joseph into slavery. Joseph is taken down to Egypt, and the brothers never expect to hear from him again.

Of course, they cannot come back to their father and tell him what really happened to his favorite son, so they must construct a lie. They must cover up their sin. They take Joseph's robe, dip it in goat blood, and lie to their father's face, telling him, "This we have found; please identify whether it is your son's robe or not" (Genesis 37:32). Jacob believes the lie, saying, "It is my son's robe. A fierce animal has devoured him. Joseph is without doubt torn to pieces" (v. 33). Jacob weeps and mourns and refuses to be comforted.

Joseph's brothers live with this lie, covering it up for years and years.

THE LIE REPEATED IN OUR WORLD

In the movie *A Christmas Story*, Ralphie Parker's two best friends, Schwartz and Flick, get into a debate as to whether a person's tongue will stick to a metal pole in the cold of an Indiana December. Schwartz says it will. Flick says it won't. So Schwartz dares (and double-dog dares and even triple-dog dares) Flick to do it, to stick his tongue to a metal pole.

When Flick does, his tongue sticks. At that moment, the bell rings and all the kids run back to class, abandoning poor Flick in the cold, his tongue firmly attached to the pole.

When their teacher asks the class where Flick is, they all sit in silence. Then she asks Ralphie directly if he has seen his friend, and Ralphie lies to her face. Ralphie was a mere bystander in the whole incident, but he still covers up what happened, betraying and abandoning his friend.

And here we find from Ralphie Parker an example of Satan's subtlety with this lie. Satan convinces us not just to cover up our sin but also to cover up and make secret anything that makes us uncomfortable, even if it is not sin.

I remember one time I had this massive pimple on my cheek. It swelled up horribly. When someone asked me what happened to my face, I said I got scratched by a cat. At the time, I did not have a cat. I did not even know anyone nearby who had a cat. I just could not bear telling this person that the swelling and redness on my face was what it was. I preferred a lie over the truth. When we are embarrassed and ashamed, we often lie to cover up the truth. And that is what makes Satan so dangerous with this lie. "You must cover up

> *When we are embarrassed and ashamed, we often lie to cover up the truth.*

your sin" leads to "You must cover up the truth" leads to "You must hide, isolate, and never trust anyone."

But lest we think this is something that only affects children, we must recognize that we continue this pattern of covering up well into adulthood.

When you make a mistake at work, that is no sin. But have you ever found a way to hide the mistake rather than confessing it? Have you perhaps found a way to blame someone else?

Have you ever made a mistake at home that you were embarrassed by? That is not necessarily sin. But have you tried to hide that mistake from your spouse because you feared they would be upset with you?

Have you ever been on a website you should not be visiting and then deleted your browser history?

This lie does some of its worst damage when church leaders abuse God's people and then other church leaders aid in concealing the abuse in order to protect the leadership. If this has ever happened to you, I am so sorry. If you have done this, repent and confess and flee from the darkness, for the light of Jesus will reveal all things.

Such situations of abuse are often paired with Lie 4 and the need to maintain control over situations. They come with the darkness of secrecy, legal battles, and nondisclosure agreements.

Covering up our sins means shrouding our sins in darkness, hiding them from others. Perhaps we wish we could hide our sin from ourselves too. The apostle John writes, "If we say we have no sin, we deceive ourselves, and the truth is not in us" (1 John 1:8). We may have temporary success in hiding our sins from ourselves or others, but Satan prizes every opportunity to remind us of our sins. Satan pushes us toward self-deception, which causes us to think that if we just ignore the problem, it will magically go away. I am a champion of this method. Let me assure you, it does not work. If we speak a hurtful word to a friend, it will not magically go away. We must repent, confess, and apologize or the sin will fester and the friendship will start to unravel. But John also assures us of this: "If we confess our sins, He is faithful and just to forgive us our sins and to cleanse us from all unrighteousness" (v. 9).

Yet we not only hide sin from others and ourselves; we also attempt to hide our sins from the light of Jesus. This never works. As John writes elsewhere, "The light shines in the darkness, and the darkness has not overcome it" (John 1:5). Darkness and all we seek to conceal there cannot remain hidden from Jesus, the light of the world.

Paul writes, "For at one time you were darkness, but now you are light in the Lord. Walk as children of light (for the fruit of light is found in all that is good and right and true)" (Ephesians 5:8–9). The fruit of light is good and right and true. The fruit of darkness is evil and wrong and lies.

THE TRUTH

Concealing the truth means placing the truth in darkness, where we think no one can see it. It means hiding the truth from the light. Jesus comes as light. He shines in our darkness. He illuminates what we wish to keep hidden. He says, "Come here. Let Me see that. Ah, let Me get rid of that for you. Don't you feel better now?"

Covering up sin is like putting a rock in your shoe on purpose, then having to pretend like nothing is wrong. The best thing to do is to just stop and take out the rock. That is what Jesus does for us. He reaches down, removes our shoes, locates and removes the rock, then washes our feet in forgiveness. For good measure, He points our feet toward delighting in His will and walking in His way of truth and light, unencumbered by secrets and lies.

The truth is, we have been clothed by Christ. In Baptism, we were clothed in the robe of Christ's righteousness. And that righteousness is not just an outer covering that hides all the garbage and sin underneath. It is not as if sin is who we truly are and Jesus is merely hiding our sin. Rather, Jesus Christ and His righteousness transform us, re-create us into new people.

Christ's robe of righteousness works for our benefit in much the same way Sauron's One Ring works for evil in J. R. R. Tolkien's *The Lord of the Rings*. Anyone who bears the ring becomes more and more like Sauron the longer they wear it. Their will is subsumed by Sauron's will. We may see glimpses of good when Bilbo, Frodo, or even Gollum seem like their old selves, but the One Ring will eventually consume anyone who wears it, causing them to bear the image of the ring's true master, Sauron.

The robe of righteousness we are given transforms us to be more and more like Jesus, to be conformed to His will. We may see glimpses of our old selves when our sin shines through, but the robe of Christ's righteousness will eventually transform us entirely and totally into the image of Jesus when He returns.

We do not have to cover up anything because we have been transformed by the righteous covering Jesus has provided for us.

> *We do not have to cover up anything because we have been transformed by the righteous covering Jesus has provided for us.*

GOD'S DESIRED OUTCOME

God's desired outcome is that we receive forgiveness. As Jesus says to Zacchaeus, "For the Son of Man came to seek and to save the lost" (Luke 19:10). Jesus wants all our sins to come to light, to be forgiven, to be covered in His righteousness rather than by a shroud of secrecy and darkness.

This does not mean that you have to share your every sin on social media. But it does mean that when you sin against particular people, you confess and ask their forgiveness. It does mean that you confess your sins before God. And if you have never participated in private confession and absolution, know that it can be a powerful and freeing experience. Many of us may be resistant to this. But there is something inescapable about hearing the words "I forgive you" when that *you* is singular instead of plural.

God desires that we receive forgiveness and live in His light. And God does not just desire this outcome. God makes it happen. When Adam and Eve fall into sin and then cover and hide themselves, God comes looking for them. God brings them back into the light, hears their confession, and promises that Satan's head will be crushed. And when it comes time for Satan's head to be crushed, God sends His own Son to do the crushing. God sends His own Son to be crushed.

As He goes to the cross for us, Jesus is stripped and uncovered to bear our sin and shame so that we might be covered and clothed in His righteousness.

THE LOVE THAT CASTS OUT FEAR

We cover up our sin because we are afraid of losing our relationships. We are afraid of being abandoned because of our mistakes. The love Jesus shows us draws near to us when we are hiding. It is no accident that the first words out of God's mouth after the fall are "Where are you?" (Genesis 3:9). God seeks us because He loves us. He loves us and takes action to save us, to restore and reconcile our relationship when we are still sinners, when we are still weak, when we are still hiding and cowering in the shadows.

Paul writes, "But God shows His love for us in that while we were still sinners, Christ died for us" (Romans 5:8). Perhaps you are familiar with that verse. But do not forget what comes after it:

> **Since, therefore, we have now been justified by His blood, much more shall we be saved by Him from the wrath of God. For if while we were enemies we were**

reconciled to God by the death of His Son, much more, now that we are reconciled, shall we be saved by His life. More than that, we also rejoice in God through our Lord Jesus Christ, through whom we have now received reconciliation. (vv. 9–11)

Our relationship with God is reconciled because of Jesus. We need not fear the wrath of God. God will not abandon us. Our relationship with God is restored by the very blood of Jesus. We are no longer God's enemies. Anything Satan tells us about needing to hide from God is a lie, for no one ever needs to hide from someone they have been reconciled with. We are justified. We are declared by Jesus' blood to be in the right, clothed in everlasting righteousness, innocence, and blessedness.

Questions for Reflection

Where do you see this lie appearing in your life?

What sins are you most tempted to cover up?

Can you remember a time when you were afraid of being abandoned? What was that like?

Whom can you trust to tell you the truth when you are struggling with this lie?

Can you think of other biblical characters who covered up their sin?

Scripture for Meditation

Genesis 3:20–21

1 John 1:7–9

Colossians 3:1–17

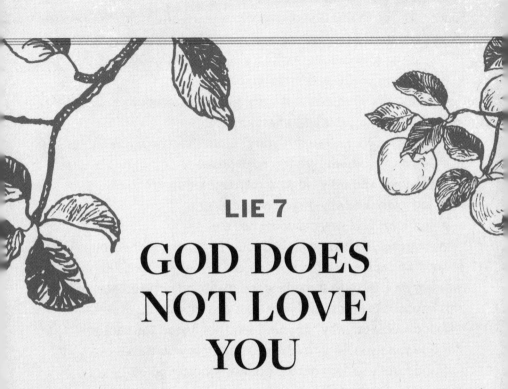

LIE 7

GOD DOES NOT LOVE YOU

Each lie that Satan tells has a way of expanding its root system into our souls. The lie that God does not love you is often felt when people have been through something traumatic. I find it often begins with an "if," a casting of doubt on God's love with a question:

If God loves you, why did this happen?

This lie takes all shapes and sizes. Anytime somebody experiences pain and suffering, this lie comes out.

If God loves you, why didn't you get into the school you wanted?

If God loves you, why are you so depressed?

If God loves you, why did your marriage fall apart?

If God loves you, why do you have cancer?

If God loves you, why did your child die?

In each case, the next sentence could be "That does not sound very loving." Of course, Satan is not content to merely shout this lie when we have gone through something traumatic and terrible. Satan will say this lie about the most everyday trials and tribulations as well.

If God loves you, why has your friend not texted you back yet?

If God loves you, why haven't you gotten any Christmas cards yet?

If God loves you, why did the hot water heater go out?

I am sure you can fill in the blank with how Satan has lied to you with this formula.

SATAN IN THE GARDEN

Genesis 3 tells us that Adam and Eve have not experienced anything other than God's love. They are familiar only with love in the perfect creation of Eden. As Satan comes to Eve, asking about God's instructions, he introduces the possibility of something other than love coming from God.

Satan proposes that perhaps God's actions toward Adam and Eve are not love. Perhaps God is being selfish. Perhaps God is holding out on Adam and Eve. Perhaps God is forcing Adam and Eve to lack what they truly need. "If God loves you, why did He withhold the knowledge of good and evil from you? Why would He withhold anything from you? Withholding things is not love."

This lie works together quite well with many of the other lies Satan weaves in the Garden of Eden. When we think God does not love us, we can be more easily persuaded to seize control (Lie 4). When we are convinced that God does not love us, we will more easily define ourselves by our performance rather than by God's love (Lie 2). When we believe God does not love us, we are left believing God will not save us and we must save ourselves (Lie 8). We are left believing that we are alone (Lie 9) and that the reason God does not love us must be that we are too flawed to be forgiven (Lie 10). Ultimately, it is not possible to trust God if we believe He does not love us.

Satan proposes that perhaps God's actions toward Adam and Eve are not love.

SATAN IN THE HEAVENLY COUNCIL

In the case of Job, Satan believes that the only reason Job fears and follows God is because God has made Job's life too easy. Satan persuades God to allow him to attack Job and make his life miserable. Once all that ease has been taken away, Satan can point to all the calamities as evidence of God's lack of love. I imagine Satan suggesting the following to Job:

If God loves you, why did you lose all your wealth, Job?

If God loves you, why did your children die, Job?

If God loves you, why are you covered head to foot in loathsome sores, Job?

If God loves you, why has your wife told you to get on with it and die already, Job?

If God loves you, why are your friends such miserable comforters, Job?

While Satan may be whispering such lies, Job's wife is the one who speaks this lie to Job: "Do you still hold fast your integrity? Curse God and die" (Job 2:9). Calling on Job to curse God is a call for Job to admit that God does not love him. Curse the One who gave you this life. Curse the One who is responsible for what happens in this world. Curse the Creator and leave His creation.

What is scary and dangerous about this line of thinking is that it is entirely logical. If God is against us, who can be for us? If the Creator hates us or is so indifferent to us that He allows us to suffer this much, then why bother living in His world?

The book of Job forces us to ask ourselves hard questions. It invites us to consider our limited ability to view and understand what God is up to. It reminds us that there are things we do not understand, things God has hidden from us. But those hidden things do not mean God does not love us.

> *There are things we do not understand, things God has hidden from us. But those hidden things do not mean God does not love us.*

In Job's story, when God shows up and reveals Himself, He restores Job's fortunes. Job's possessions and wealth are doubled. The only thing Job had lost that is not numerically doubled in the restoration are the number of his children. He had ten before the tragedy. He has ten after the tragedy. He had seven sons and three daughters before the tragedy and seven sons and three daughters after the tragedy. I wonder if perhaps this detail is hinting at the resurrection of the dead. This could happen in two ways. In one sense, if Job has ten more children, then the number of his children does double, for his children who died in the tragedy will rise from the grave. Job's children are then doubled from ten to twenty. The other possibility is that Job's children were simply raised from the dead.[12] Whatever the case, God shows great love to Job in the abundant restoration.

Satan does not want Job to see the days ahead. Satan wants Job to curse God and die in misery, without all things being restored and made new. Satan wants Job and you and me to look at all tragedies and traumas with as shortsighted a view as possible, so that we despair of life and never see the fruition of what God is up to.

SATAN'S DESIRED OUTCOME

When Satan tells his lies, he desires several possible outcomes. At its core, this lie that God does not love you seeks to rob you of love, joy, and assurance. This lie introduces and fixates us on the possibility of problems. Satan wants us worrying and overanalyzing everything. Satan desires that our uncertainty makes us anxious, that our anxiety makes us miserable, and that our misery spreads and clouds out any joy or love that seeks us. Satan wants us stuck in the difficulties of the present, unable to imagine any hope for a better future. And Satan wants us stuck in worry about the difficulties of the future, unable to enjoy any of the delights of our present situations.

For many of us, much of the time, this lie stays in the territory of anxious worry and uncomfortable uncertainty. We have miserable days, but the love of friends and family, along with the love of Jesus, shine through, and the fog and clouds of misery dissipate.

For some people, however, this lie leads to misery that lasts not for a matter of days but for much of their lives. The extreme end of such misery is despair and, ultimately, if Satan can manage it, an expedited death. Like he did with Job, Satan wants to produce so much suffering and misery in our lives that the pain of continuing to live is unbearable.

However deep into the darkness of misery Satan takes us, he will press us to blame God for our pain and suffering. And if God is to

---

12 For more of a discussion on this topic, see Horace Hummel's *The Word Becoming Flesh* (St. Louis: Concordia Publishing House, 1979), 488.

blame, then God does not love us. How could God love us and let us endure this? And if God does not love us, what is the point of living?

This leads many people to another outcome Satan desires in telling this lie: disbelief and the abandonment of God.

THE FEAR BEHIND THE LIE

In this case, the fear behind the lie is the lie itself. Satan simply names the deep, dark fear that we are unwanted and unlovable. In our day-to-day lives, many of our relationships are negatively affected by this fear. We may not feel appreciated by our family. We may feel like we are overlooked and not needed by our circle of friends. We may wonder if anybody would even notice if we stopped showing up at church.

> *Satan simply names the deep, dark fear that we are unwanted and unlovable.*

Satan certainly preys on this fear in our relationships, but he is always aiming higher, always seeking to persuade us that God does not love us. Our lives can quickly become a mess from fractured relationships with friends and family. Our friendships may grow or fade, break or blossom. They may die and decay, and new friendships arise instead.

But when our relationship with God is broken, there is no replacing it. There is no moving on to anything comparable. If we are persuaded that we are unloved and unwanted by God so that we abandon Him, we transfer ourselves out of the kingdom of light and back into the domain of darkness.

Satan wants us to steep in this fear of being unloved. He wants us to repeat it to ourselves again and again. Satan wants us saying, "Nobody loves me," as a mantra all day, every day. He wants us to abandon our friendships. He wants family fractures to remain unrepaired. Satan wants us to look around at our lives and the world and see only brokenness. And with the evidence of everything else broken, Satan then points us heavenward and lies, "Yeah, it's just as bad up there with God. Why would God, who created this mess, be any different than the mess itself?"

We pray in the Lord's Prayer, "Your will be done, on earth as it is in heaven" (Matthew 6:10). Satan seeks to reverse this prayer and aim it at himself. Satan wants his own will to be done in heaven as it is on earth. He wants us to believe not only that we are unlovable but also that the earth itself is unredeemable and unlovable.

In a world where we can instantaneously see devastation happening around the globe, Satan wants us to believe that the whole of God's creation is unloved and unlovable. For then we will not only fear that we are unlovable but also cease to love others.

THE LIE REPEATED IN THE BIBLE

GIDEON

In Judges 6, the people of Israel are under the tyranny of the Midianites. The Midianites and their allies keep stealing all the Israelites' crops and cattle. God's people are forced to hide in caves and eke out a living.

The angel of the Lord appears to Gideon, saying, "The LORD is with you, O mighty man of valor" (Judges 6:12). Gideon replies with one of the saddest, most relatable lines in all the Scriptures, "Please, my lord, if the LORD is with us, why then has all this happened to us?" (v. 13).

If the Lord is with us, why are all these bad things happening? If the Lord loves us, why has He forsaken us?

Gideon's question is not answered. Rather, the Lord promises His presence with Gideon and sends Gideon out to deliver Israel from the hand of Midian. The Lord keeps His promise of presence. He shows Gideon signs to assure him of His presence. In the end, Gideon delivers Israel in such a way that God's continued guidance and presence is the only explanation for the victory.

JESUS ON THE CROSS

As Jesus is crucified, He suffers through much physical pain and agony. He suffers through the pain of being betrayed by Judas, denied by Peter, and abandoned by His closest friends. And Jesus endures taunts and verbal abuse from the soldiers, crowds, and religious leaders. This is one example of what the chief priests say to Jesus while He is dying on the cross:

> **He saved others; He cannot save Himself. He is the King of Israel; let Him come down now from the cross, and we will believe in Him. He trusts in God; let God deliver Him now, if He desires Him. For He said, "I am the Son of God." (Matthew 27:42–43)**

As Jesus dies for the sins of the world, including the sins of the very people hurling insults at Him, He is told this chapter's lie. God does not love You, Jesus. If God loved You, would You really be up there on the cross dying? The evidence backs up the lie. A bystander would probably view Jesus as someone who was despised, rejected, hated.

The Scriptures record God the Father speaking of His love for His Son. At Jesus' Baptism, we hear, "This is My beloved Son, with whom I am well pleased" (Matthew 3:17).

We also hear God the Father speak something quite similar at Jesus' transfiguration: "This is My beloved Son, with whom I am well pleased; listen to Him" (Matthew 17:5).

Likewise, Jesus speaks of the love of His Father to His disciples, saying, "As the Father has loved Me, so have I loved you. Abide in My love" (John 15:9). Jesus says this to His disciples mere hours before the chief priests hurl Satan's lie at Him on the cross.

Even when He is dying, Jesus says, "Father, forgive them, for they know not what they do" (Luke 23:34). Jesus shows love, mercy, and forgiveness as He dies in agony.

And there is one bystander we hear from, a Roman centurion, who observes something different after Jesus dies: "Truly this man was the Son of God!" (Mark 15:39).

When you must endure Satan's lie that God does not love you, remember that Jesus endured that lie as well. Jesus understands. And Jesus is risen from the dead. We follow Jesus. We follow Him while harmed and harassed by Satan's lies. We follow Him into death. And we follow Him into the resurrection and eternal life.

> *When you must endure Satan's lie that God does not love you, remember that Jesus endured that lie as well.*

THE LIE REPEATED IN OUR WORLD

Many people will point to the irrational suffering present in the world as their reason for disbelief in God. They ask why God would create creatures that seemingly have no purpose but to inflict horrifying pain. They ask why God would allow bone cancer in children. These are good questions. We must admit that such questions about pain and suffering often leave us Christians sounding a lot like Job's three friends in our answers, spewing out foolish clichés that blame suffering on those who are suffering.

Or such questions about pain and suffering force Christians to simply say, "I don't know." And for many, that is not a satisfactory answer.

Why did I lose my job? I don't know.

Why did I have a miscarriage? I don't know.

Why did my church abuse me and then not believe me? I don't know.

I do not possess a perfect answer to any of these questions. I know Satan uses such suffering to push people away from God. I know God dwells with us in the suffering. But I do not have a silver bullet answer that will persuade people to faith and trust in Jesus. I do hope that my response in the next section will be helpful for those who struggle mightily with suffering and with the lie that God does not love them.

THE TRUTH

The apostle Paul understood suffering. He gives a laundry list of his sufferings in 2 Corinthians, including "afflictions, hardships, calamities, beatings, imprisonments, riots, labors, sleepless nights, hunger" (6:4–5). And yet this same person who endured all that also tells us: "For I consider that the sufferings of this present time are not worth comparing with the glory that is to be revealed to us" (Romans 8:18). Yes, the sufferings of this present world are awful, terrible, beyond sense and reason. But we believe even these horrific sufferings are not worth comparing to the glory that awaits us. As bad as life can be on earth, and it can be unbearable, so much better will eternal life be in the new creation.

Later in the same chapter of Romans, Paul also speaks of creation being in bondage to corruption, subjected to the futility we see and feel in suffering. Paul writes, "For we know that the whole creation has been groaning together in the pains of childbirth until now. And not only the creation, but we ourselves, who have the firstfruits of the Spirit, groan inwardly as we wait eagerly for adoption as sons, the redemption of our bodies" (vv. 22–23).

We eagerly await the return of Jesus and the resurrection to eternal life, the redemption and perfection and glorification of our bodies. In Baptism, we were adopted into God's family. He claimed us as His own. But though we belong to Him, we spend our lives in the orphanage of the old earth, in a creation subjected to futility and in bondage to corruption. We await the day when Jesus will arrive and bring our true home down to us, re-creating creation, freeing it from futility, cutting it loose from corruption.

And yet we must admit that this is a hope that we do not see. What we see is the suffering, the pain, the violence of our world. Paul once again: "But if we hope for what we do not see, we wait for it with patience" (v. 25).

Likewise the author of Hebrews writes, "Now faith is the assurance of things hoped for, the conviction of things not seen" (Hebrews 11:1).

When we look at the suffering of the world, it is hard to see any reason to hope. It is hard to remember that God does actually love us when we see all of

We await the day when Jesus will arrive and bring our true home down to us.

creation's corruption. It is hard to recall God's love when we cannot understand the point or purpose of the world's suffering.

But when we look to Jesus, we see love. Jesus cares about our well-being. We see in His ministry countless examples where He frees people from suffering. He casts out demonic forces. He heals diseases. He heals those who are lame and paralyzed so that they walk home. He opens the eyes of the blind. He even raises people from the dead.

Jesus encounters many people who are suffering, whose circumstances look like evidence that they are unloved and unlovable. But our circumstances are not evidence of a lack of God's love. Nothing can separate us from God's love. Our hope is placed in what we do not see—in the resurrected Savior, who will bring about a world where no one suffers pain, despair, or abuse, a world where everyone is free from cancer, Alzheimer's, and multiple sclerosis. We await a world where nothing is futile and no one is corrupted. We await a world that nobody could ever even complain about, where grief is impossible and joy is unavoidable.

The truth is that Jesus chose to come into this world where unthinkable suffering occurs. He chose to become a vulnerable human being who endured that suffering not only *for* us but also *with* us. The truth is that He chose to do this out of love for the world. He chose to come down to earth and suffer, die, and rise again for the healing and restoration of this broken world, to bring an end to its futility, to restore it to a glory that far surpasses the suffering.

GOD'S DESIRED OUTCOME

God's desired outcome is that we bask in His love, abide in His love, take comfort in His love for all our days. Satan desires our misery, despair, disbelief, and death. God desires our joy, hope, faith, and eternal life. God's desired outcome is to bring us into eternal life so that we see the promised glory that awaits us. God desires the redemption, resurrection, and re-creation of our bodies. And God will bring about His desired outcome when Jesus returns.

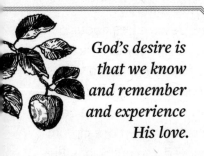

God's desire is that we know and remember and experience His love.

God wants you to know that He loves you. God wants all people to know that He loves them. He loves the world. God's desire is that we know and remember and experience His love. Jesus gave His people tangible reminders of His love that we still experience today. In Baptism, God uses simple water and the spectacular promise of His Word to forgive our sin, to place His triune name upon us, and to bring us into His family. In the Lord's Supper, Jesus utilizes commonplace bread and wine to prepare the most magnificent feast of forgiveness and life. Jesus proclaims this bread is His body given for you; this wine is His blood shed for your forgiveness. Jesus initiates these sacraments and celebrations to forgive us and remind us of His love for us. Jesus invites us, "Do this in remembrance of Me" (Luke 22:19). When you receive the Lord's Supper, when you remember your Baptism, remember the great love that Jesus has for you. Remember that He enters into your suffering. Remember that He will deliver you from your suffering. Remember that He will bring you into an eternal life free from suffering.

As we remember God's love to us, God's love leads us to love others. The apostle John writes this: "Beloved, let us love one another, for love is from God, and whoever loves has been born of God and knows God. Anyone who does not love does not know God, because God is love" (1 John 4:7–8).

Jesus says this to His disciples: "This is My commandment, that you love one another as I have loved you" (John 15:12).

God is love. He shows His love to us in Jesus' incarnation, death, and resurrection. God desires that we bask in that love, that we let it permeate, surround, and fill us so that His love overflows from us out to others.

God is love, and He loves us so much that He desires that we become love as well.

THE LOVE THAT CASTS OUT FEAR

A promise I read with frequency to people who are homebound, grieving, or nearing death is found at the end of Romans 8. Paul writes,

> **For I am sure that neither death nor life, nor angels nor rulers, nor things present nor things to come, nor powers, nor height nor depth, nor anything else in all creation, will be able to separate us from the love of God in Christ Jesus our Lord.** (Romans 8:38–39)

Nothing can separate us from the love of God. Nothing.

Satan's lies cannot separate us from the love of God. Loss of wealth, loss of health, and even the loss of people we love cannot separate us from the love of God. Death cannot separate us from God's love shown to us in Jesus.

The love that God lavishes on us transforms us from His rebellious enemies to His beloved children. John writes, "See what kind of love the Father has given to us, that we should be called children of God;

and so we are" (1 John 3:1). You are God's beloved child. You are made so by His love.

One of my favorite hymns begins with these words:

> My song is love unknown,
> My Savior's love to me,
> Love to the loveless shown
> That they might lovely be.[13]

We are made lovely by the love we are shown in Jesus. This love creates and re-creates us to be God's people. This love is yours.

Your life may be unbearably challenging right now. You may find yourself like Job, having lost everything, in pain and anguish beyond words. You may wish to simply give up. You may have read this chapter thinking that all this talk about love is nonsense.

I assure you it is not. Jesus loves you. And whatever you have lost, whatever suffering and misery and darkness you currently endure, it will not be worth comparing to the comfort and joy and light that awaits.

Questions for Reflection

Where do you see this lie appearing in your life?

---

13 Samuel Crossman, "My Song Is Love Unknown," *Lutheran Service Book* 430:1.

In what situations do you find it most difficult to see God's love?

Can you remember a time when you were afraid that you were not loved? What was that like?

Whom can you trust to tell you the truth when you are struggling with this lie?

Can you think of other biblical characters who felt unloved and unlovable?

Scripture for Meditation

Psalm 13

Lamentations 3:19–24

Romans 5:1–8

John 15:1–17

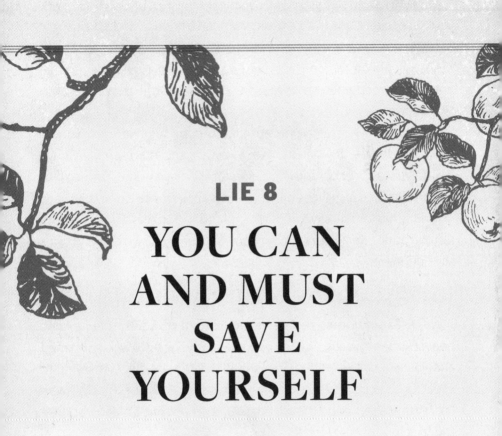

LIE 8

YOU CAN AND MUST SAVE YOURSELF

This lie takes on so many subtle shades in the lives of God's people. If you were to take a poll of Christians around the world and ask outright, "Who is your Savior?" I do not know what results you would get. I hope "Jesus" would be the only answer. I do know that even if we get that answer correct when surveyed, we all struggle to live according to that answer.

Sometimes we struggle because life is good and we have worked hard to cultivate the life we have. We want credit for what we have built. We want recognition for how far we have come. Sometimes we struggle because life is difficult and it appears like there is nobody else who can or will save us, so it's up to us. For reasons of desperation or pride, we all struggle with the thought that we can and must save ourselves.

SATAN IN THE GARDEN

When Satan comes to Eve in the Garden of Eden, this lie lurks beneath these words: "When you eat of it your eyes will be opened, and you will be like God" (Genesis 3:5). Satan, in effect, is saying to Eve, "If you want to escape from the tyrannical rule of this God who has withheld this good thing from you, then you must reach out, take the fruit, and save yourself."

Satan convinces Adam and Eve to try to save themselves from a perfect creation and a perfect Creator. How treacherous is that? Satan persuades them it is not a perfect creation, that they are not perfect creatures. They are lacking this knowledge. They need it. God will not give it to them, so they must take hold of it on their own. They must save themselves.

The lie pushes Adam and Eve away from God and toward reliance on self. One aspect of the curse of the fall is that we remain susceptible to wanting self-reliance and independence. In my experience (and perhaps in yours), independence is equated with strength. Dependence is equated with weakness. This is a lie. We were created to be in a trusting, dependent relationship with God.

SATAN IN THE WILDERNESS

This lie lurks beneath two of the temptations Satan uses against Jesus. The words "command these stones to become loaves of bread" (Matthew 4:3) come with the backdrop of "You're hungry. Save Yourself from that hunger. It'll be easy if You are who God says You are."

> *We were created to be in a trusting, dependent relationship with God.*

Satan again tempts Jesus, saying, "All these [earthly kingdoms] I will give You, if You will fall down and worship me" (v. 9). Satan may as well have said, "Don't bother with the cross. Don't risk death. Don't rely on God to raise You from the dead, Jesus. Just bend the knee and all this will be Yours. Save Yourself."

The first temptation offers independence as the way forward. The other temptation offers the path of least resistance as the way forward, which in this case means dependence on someone other than God. Conveniently for Satan, that someone is himself. Satan is so arrogant, he proposes himself as savior to the Savior of the world.

When Satan tells Jesus this lie, it hits a bit different than with us. Jesus is the Savior of the world. We are not. Satan tells Jesus to save Himself from the very act of saving us. Jesus could have saved Himself but chose to save us. We cannot save ourselves. We have no hope of that.

Whether Satan is lying to Jesus or to you and me, his goal is to separate us from our heavenly Father.

SATAN'S DESIRED OUTCOME

Satan's first desired outcome with this lie is to drive a wedge between us and God. Satan wants us to stop looking to God for all good and start looking elsewhere. The very act of looking elsewhere is an act of rebellion, an act of independence. As we look away from God, we assert our own dominion.

In the garden, in the wilderness, and in all its repetitions, this lie interplays with Lie 1. As Satan tries to separate us from God, Satan does not want us to trust God or rely on Him. Satan wants us to rely on ourselves or anything that is not God. When we fall into trouble and need help, our valuing of independence means we will try to get out of the mess on our own. We may hide or cover ourselves with fig leaves. We may blame others or tell a few lies ourselves to find a way out of trouble, to save ourselves.

Once Satan gets us asserting our independence from God, we will see everything as our responsibility. Satan will play to our egos and attract us to the idea of getting credit for doing things on our own. We will not trust God or anyone else to help us. But Satan will also burden us with the enormity of being independent so that we feel overwhelmed by such massive responsibility.

The lie "You must save yourself" works much better when we have already bought Lie 1, that we cannot trust God. Likewise, the lie "You can save yourself" leads us to think we do not need God and therefore have no need of trusting Him.

> *Satan wants nothing more than for his lie to become our truth, for us to seek salvation in and from ourselves.*

When that wedge of distrust has been placed between us and God, Satan's desired outcome is that we give this lie a try. Satan wants nothing more than for his lie to become our truth, for us to seek salvation in and from ourselves. Satan has been telling people that they must save themselves for centuries. And Satan knows that they have all failed.

Each one has sinned. Each one has died (minus a couple of anomalies, such as Enoch and Elijah[14]). Each one remained dead.

But in the wilderness, Satan sees Jesus threatening to turn everything right side up again. If Jesus suffers, dies, and rises, then salvation will come from Him. All those faithful people of days past who could not save themselves, who died before their eyes beheld salvation, will rise with Jesus to everlasting life. Jesus' death and resurrection will prove Satan a liar once and for all. Because you cannot save yourself. Only Jesus can save you, and He has.

Satan loves this lie because inside of it are two massively potent lies: first, that somehow we can indeed save ourselves by our own performance (pushing us back to Lie 2), and second, that since we have not been successful at saving ourselves, we are therefore damned (pushing us ahead to Lie 10). If we think we can save ourselves, we will keep looking to ourselves and our own works and wonders all the time. We will keep our eyes fixed on ourselves, hoping that we will author and edit our own salvation story. The lie becomes "You must save yourself . . . and you can do it, if you just try a little harder."

If we swallow the lie that we must save ourselves, we will constantly be pushing and striving and trying harder and harder, all the while feeling worse and worse about our chances of being saved. Then Satan comes with a steady dose of the simple truth. Because the truth is we have not done and cannot do enough to be saved. The lie then becomes "You must save yourself . . . and you can't . . . which means you are doomed and damned."

Satan's desired outcome is that we will hope in ourselves (or anything other than Jesus); this false hope will rightly lead us to despair because there is no way for us to do enough. Because of Adam and Eve's fall into sin, there is no possibility of living a sinless life for any person, save Jesus.

14 For more on Enoch, see Genesis 5:21–24. For more on Elijah, see 2 Kings 2:1–14.

Satan can fill in anything after the lie and push and prod us to all sorts of falsehoods. You must save yourself . . . which means your neighbor must save herself and you can ignore her. You must save yourself . . . and you hated your neighbor instead of helping her, so you're doomed. You must save yourself . . . but God will be an easy grader, so go ahead and indulge that sin. You must save yourself . . . but you definitely overindulged on that sin, and God won't forgive that. All these are lies.

Satan loves this lie because he can end the sentence with whatever he wants and then throw the opposite at us with just as much effect and power. It is a lie pendulum that keeps ticking back and forth between lies.

Another desired outcome with this lie is that Satan wants us to repeat this lie to one another. (We will see this with Simon Peter below.) In cultures that place a high value on independence, Satan has much success in getting people to repeat this lie for him.

How often have people who are addicted been told to "fix yourself"? How often have people who are homeless or unemployed been told to "get a job"? How often have those who are poor and hungry been ignored to the tune of "What is that to me?"

I find myself complicit in this lie when I encounter sin that I find particularly egregious. I am tempted to abandon murderers, Ponzi schemers, and sex offenders to suffer the consequences of the state.

I am forced to pause and consider how often the words the chief priests said to Judas—"What is that to us? See to it yourself" (Matthew 27:4)—have been my thoughts, my words, my actions.

Far, far too often. Satan's desired outcome becomes reality every time we repeat this lie for him, every time we call on others to save themselves.

THE FEAR BEHIND THE LIE

As there are multiple outcomes to this lie, so there are multiple fears behind it. When we realize that we cannot save ourselves, Satan preys on our fear of being incompetent, stupid, and helpless. Whether at school, work, or home, none of us likes feeling stupid. We will often go to extreme lengths to prove that we are competent.

As we set to the task of proving our brilliance and ability, we often become overwhelmed with the enormity of the task. Satan preys on that fear, the fear that the task is too great for us, too big for us. And if the task is too big, if we cannot accomplish it, then we will be proven incompetent.

But the other fear that I see lurking beneath this lie is the fear of being invaded and overtaken and thus losing a sense of purpose and meaning. Since I cannot save myself and must be saved by another, well, what good am I?

The fears of being incompetent, overwhelmed, and invaded all lead to feelings of uselessness. What do we do with useless things? We throw them away. I have never met anyone who enjoys feeling useless or wants to be thrown away. Have you?

> *The fears of being incompetent, overwhelmed, and invaded all lead to feelings of uselessness.*

THE LIE REPEATED IN THE BIBLE

JUDAS ISCARIOT

One of the most tragic characters in the Scriptures is Judas Iscariot. Judas was a thief and a liar. Satan had much sway and influence over him. In John 12:1–8, just before Palm Sunday in John's telling, Jesus is eating at the house of Mary, Martha, and Lazarus (who had just been raised from the dead) in Bethany. Mary takes an excessive amount of expensive ointment and anoints Jesus' feet. This causes Judas to grumble, "Why was this ointment not sold for three hundred denarii and given to the poor?" (John 12:5). A denarius was worth about a day's wages for a laborer. So imagine a perfume worth a year's salary being used up in one action. How much Chanel No. 5 would it take to be worth a year's wages?[15]

But John reveals to us that Judas's intentions were not honorable. John writes that Judas says this "not because he cared about the poor, but because he was a thief, and having charge of the moneybag he used to help himself to what was put into it" (v. 6).

Judas is so angered by Mary's actions and Jesus' response that he goes to the chief priests and offers to betray Jesus into their hands. The chief priests have been searching for an opportunity to arrest Jesus, but they have not been able to because of the crowds surrounding Jesus all the time. But now they have their chance to do it by stealth at night with no crowd to protect Jesus. It's an inside job.

Judas procures a band of soldiers and brings them to arrest Jesus. Jesus is first put on trial before the chief priests. They find Jesus guilty. Here is what Matthew tells us: "When morning came, all the chief priests and the elders of the people took counsel against Jesus to put Him to death. And they bound Him and led Him away and delivered Him over to Pilate the governor" (Matthew 27:1–2).

It's at this point in Judas's story when he has an encounter that seals his fate. Matthew writes, "Then when Judas, His betrayer, saw that Jesus was condemned, he changed his mind and brought back the thirty pieces of silver to the chief priests and the elders" (v. 3).

That one line is haunting to me: "he changed his mind." Judas is before the chief priests and the elders, and he confesses, "I have sinned by betraying innocent blood" (v. 4a)

But then Judas hears a lie from Satan. This lie is not internal, not from his own marred soul and mind. Judas hears a lie from Satan out of the mouths of the chief priests. Judas hears Satan lying through the very mouths of those who ought to have reminded him of God's

---

15 As of this publication, a standard hundred-milliliter bottle of Chanel No. 5 Eau de Parfum spray sells for $172. The federal minimum wage in the United States is $7.25 per hour, which comes to $58 per day. In three hundred days, that's $17,400, which could purchase about a hundred bottles of Chanel No. 5. That's ten liters, or about 2.6 gallons. In case you were wondering.

steadfast love and mercy. They tell Judas, "What is that to us? See to it yourself" (v. 4b).

These chief priests tell Judas that he is responsible for his own sin and his own salvation. "See to it yourself." They tell Judas that he must save himself from his betrayal.

Sadly for Judas, he believes this lie, and Satan pushes Judas to despair. Judas believes he has out-sinned God's grace. Judas believes he is

> *Judas hears Satan lying through the very mouths of those who ought to have reminded him of God's steadfast love and mercy.*

beyond hope for betraying Jesus, the divine Son of God, to death. Judas has murdered God. What sin could be worse than that? Judas sees to this heinous sin himself and takes the only punishment he can see that will fit the sin: he dies by suicide.

I often wonder how the story might have played out differently if Judas had just waited until Sunday, or if Judas had turned to Jesus instead of the chief priests, but such things are hidden from us. We simply do not know what would have happened.

SATAN LIES THROUGH SIMON PETER

Satan wants us to try to save ourselves, which we cannot do. He also wants Jesus to save Himself from accomplishing the act of salvation through His death and resurrection. Satan attempts to get Jesus off mission in the temptation account in Matthew 4:1–11, but Satan does not give up there. Satan placed a lie in Peter's mouth a bit later in the story.

There had been a lot of speculation as to Jesus' identity. Jesus asks His disciples, "Who do people say that the Son of Man is?" (Matthew 16:13). They tell Him about the rumors going around that He is one of the prophets, like Elijah, Jeremiah, or John the Baptist. Jesus then asks, "But who do you say that I am?" (v. 15). Simon Peter replies, "You are the Christ, the Son of the living God" (v. 16).

After Simon Peter's correct confession, Jesus decides it is time to let His disciples in on the plan. He begins "to show His disciples that He must go to Jerusalem and suffer many things from the elders and chief priests and scribes, and be killed, and on the third day be raised" (v. 21). That is the salvation plan. Jesus will suffer, die, and rise.

But as soon as this is revealed, Satan is right there. After hearing the plan as clear as day from Jesus' own mouth, Satan shows up in Simon Peter's words and actions. Peter takes Jesus aside and rebukes Him, saying, "Far be it from You, Lord! This shall never happen to You" (v. 22).

Satan wants Jesus to save Himself so that He will not save us. So Satan gets Simon Peter to repeat this lie for him. Simon Peter, the one to whom God just revealed the truth about Jesus' identity—even he repeats this lie. Satan, speaking through Peter, proclaims, "You must save Yourself from all that trouble, Jesus."

Jesus points out what is happening for us. He tells Peter, "Get behind Me, Satan! You are a hindrance to Me. For you are not setting your mind on the things of God, but on the things of man" (v. 23).

THE LIE REPEATED IN OUR WORLD

This lie plays out in so many ways. Sometimes the result is shame. As Satan tells me that I must save myself, I feel a crushing sense of unworthiness. I am responsible, but I am going to fail. It is going to be all my fault that I experience condemnation. I no longer feel guilty for my sins, but I internalize them. My sin is who I am. And I cannot stop it. So I am condemned. All these shame-filled thoughts are lies.

Satan often tells this lie in two parts. Satan begins by holding a mirror before us—but not just any mirror. Satan holds up a false mirror that distorts reality and covers up our flaws, making us think we look quite nice. With this mirror, he tells this lie: "You can save yourself, and look, you are doing pretty well for yourself." But then, at an opportune time of weakness, Satan holds up a true mirror before us that shows us our sinful self in all its ugliness. With this true mirror, Satan then tells this lie: "You must save yourself. But look at the mess you are. Think of all the terrible things you have done." Satan rubs our noses in our sin like a cruel pet owner rubbing a dog's face in its own poop. Satan wants to embarrass and shame us. And he wants us to have crap on our face.

Personally, the lie that I must save myself gets wrapped up in Lie 2, that my value is based on my performance. When the COVID-19 pandemic began, I put so much pressure on myself. I knew the uncertainty of the pandemic was going to be challenging for people. And I could see how the differing responses from governing authorities were causing massive division throughout the country and the world. Satan's lie to me was that I must do everything right to save my congregation. I had to be perfect in how I worded everything, or people would leave the church. I had to come up with the most brilliant solutions to our restrictions, or people would leave the church. I worked so hard and was so careful—and things went well. Dare I say, things were going better in my congregation than any other I was aware of. And this supposed success went to my head, inflating my ego. Satan showed me the false mirror that made it seem like I was doing great.

It wasn't until I myself became sick with COVID-19 that Satan decided to hold up the true mirror. As I sat in our guest bedroom, mind swimming in brain fog, a woman who had been a member of my congregation since 1946 was hospitalized and dying. And I could not go visit her. I called the hospital and talked to the chaplain there, explaining the situation through tears, sniffles, and coughs. I was helpless. I could not do what my congregation had called me to do. I took it hard. My pride transitioned quickly to shame. Shame in my weakness and failures. Shame in the pride I had succumbed to. I was a mess. I could not save anyone. I could not save myself. God deserved all the credit for the growth He had given. I, who merely planted seeds and watered them, was a lowly servant.

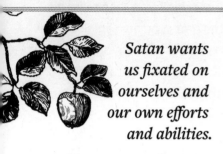

Satan wants us fixated on ourselves and our own efforts and abilities.

Satan repeats the lie of "You can and must save yourself" with variations that are particularly deadly. Satan often twists this lie in opposite directions. On the one hand, Satan says, "You can save yourself, and if you just work a bit harder, if you just put in a bit more effort, you'll get there!" Satan wants us fixated on ourselves and our own efforts and abilities. Satan wants us to believe that we can earn our way into God's favor and God's kingdom, because if we believe that lie, we will never come to understand grace. We will never understand the character of God in Christ. We will never look to Jesus.

But on the other hand, Satan varies this lie in the opposite direction. Satan says, "You must save yourself, which means you are doomed, damned, and dead already, so just give up." This often leads to an adjacent lie related to out-sinning God's grace (see Lie 10) or exempting ourselves from that grace (see Lie 5).

THE TRUTH

When I was attending the seminary, I remember being assigned to lead a midweek Lenten service. The services in this particular year were focused on the words of Jesus from the cross. I was assigned Jesus' words to the thief on the cross: "Truly, I say to you, today you will be with Me in paradise" (Luke 23:43). To tell the story, though, I took the perspective of the other thief on the cross, the thief who, when judged by his words alone, seems to make a strangely faithful confession: "Are You not the Christ? Save Yourself and us!" (v. 39). Of course, Luke tells us that this thief is railing at Jesus with these words rather than confessing with them. The forgiven thief is the one with the true confession: "Jesus, remember me when You come into Your kingdom" (v. 42).

The rebuked and railing thief was thinking only of earthly reprieve, not of eternal salvation. Yet sometimes when I hear those words, I cannot help but wonder at them. I think this thief is a great example of what it looks like to know beyond a shadow of a doubt that we cannot save ourselves. This thief understands that his salvation—even if merely a reprieve—depends on another, depends on Jesus. This thief knows that salvation, if it is going to come at all for him, must be external. He cannot save himself.

For many of us, such extreme experiences of helplessness and dependence are not memories we wish to return to. Yet these are the moments when we sit at the desk of dependence and learn our own limitations. When Satan tells us, "You must save yourself," he is lying. The truth is we must *be* saved. The truth is Jesus must save us.

This is why God sent Jesus: to save you. Jesus suffered, died, rose from the dead, ascended in power, and will return soon in that same power for you, for your salvation.

You cannot out-sin God's grace. Jesus' blood covers all sin.

> *The truth is we must be saved. The truth is Jesus must save us.*

No matter how hard you try, you cannot save yourself. You are not responsible for your own salvation, and that is good news.

Earlier, I mentioned Satan holding up false and true mirrors to us. Jesus holds up a mirror to us as well. The mirror Jesus holds up for us is one that shows our truest saintly selves, made holy not by our own actions but by Jesus' actions. This mirror perpetually shows us the cross and the risen Jesus. It shows us an image of who we were created to be and who we will be in eternity when Jesus returns and raises us from the dead. The mirror Jesus holds up shows us what it looks like to be created in God's image, after His own likeness. Yes, in this world, we will mar that image with our sin, but the mirror is not lying to us. It is showing us the truth: we are forgiven, righteous, holy, and perfect because Jesus saved us.

GOD'S DESIRED OUTCOME

God's desired outcome is that we trust in Jesus to save us, that we recognize that we cannot save ourselves. God desires that we lay down our need for independence and depend on Him.

Jesus tells us in John 15:4–5, "As the branch cannot bear fruit by itself, unless it abides in the vine, neither can you, unless you abide in Me. I am the vine; you are the branches." Branches cannot survive when detached from the vine. An independent branch is a dead branch. Branches must remain with the vine in order to live, thrive, and bear fruit. Jesus wants us to remain with Him, abide in Him, depend on Him as a branch depends on a vine.

> *Jesus' invitation to dependence does not make us useless at all; rather, we find our identity and purpose in our dependence on Him.*

And Jesus wants us to bear fruit. Satan desires that we see ourselves as useless. But Jesus' invitation to dependence does not make us useless at all; rather, we find our identity and purpose in our dependence on Him. As branches attached to the true vine, Jesus, we bear fruit. God's desired outcome is that we would bear much fruit, that we would have abundant lives, that we would abide in His love and love one another.

THE LOVE THAT CASTS OUT FEAR

You are a branch attached to the true vine, Jesus. You need not fear being too incompetent to save yourself. Jesus has saved you. You need not fear being useless. Jesus loves you. As the vine, Jesus pours His love into your life, nourishing you and enabling you to bear good fruit.

Attached to Jesus, you are not incompetent. You are not stupid. You are not useless. Jesus has created you and re-created you to grow and bear much fruit. Satan cannot invade and overwhelm you. The gates of hell will not prevail against you or anyone in Jesus' church. You are safe, protected, and so important because you are in Jesus, the vine.

Questions for Reflection

Where do you see this lie appearing in your life?

In what situations do you find yourself tempted to believe you are able to save yourself?

Can you remember a time when you were afraid of being incompetent? What was that like?

Whom can you trust to tell you the truth when you are struggling with this lie?

Can you think of other biblical characters who tried to save themselves?

Scripture for Meditation

Psalm 146

Romans 8:1–11

Acts 4:1–12

LIE 9

YOU ARE ALONE

Do you like being alone? Or are you terrified of being alone? When you hear the word *alone*, do you think of it as an enjoyable solitude or as an unbearable isolation or something in between?

God and Satan both encourage time away from other people, but for opposite reasons. God encourages us toward solitude, toward times of stillness and calm with Him and Him alone. Satan encourages us to isolate, to push others away, to hide who we truly are and what we are truly feeling from everyone, including God and even ourselves.

I find that, when we are by ourselves, solitude seems to occur when we recognize God's presence, whereas isolation occurs when we forget God's presence. Solitude can strengthen us. Isolation can only weaken us.

The lie of "you are alone" is not about solitude. This lie always leads us to isolation. Satan wants us to forget that God is always with us, that this lie can never be true. And Satan uses this lie when we are experiencing the vulnerability of grief and loss, driving us deeper into sorrow and despair.

SATAN IN THE GARDEN

In Genesis 3, it is unclear how near to each other Adam and Eve are when Satan comes in all his craftiness. Eve eats of the forbidden fruit and then gives some to Adam immediately after. We are not told if this is a walk across the garden or a simple turning around in place. However, the text tells us that Satan is speaking to Eve and Eve alone, as the text records, "He said to the woman" (Genesis 3:1). Satan isolates Eve in his address, whether or not Adam can overhear.

A strange aloneness occurs when God comes looking for Adam and Eve. God asks, "Where are you?" (v. 9). Adam replies, "I heard the sound of You in the garden, and I was afraid, because I was naked, and I hid myself" (v. 10).

Both Adam and Eve hear God in the garden. They both are afraid. They both are naked. They both hide. Yet Adam speaks only for himself here. There are few things more pleasant to Satan's ears than the first-person singular. *I*. *Me*. *Myself*.

Very little dialogue is recorded from Adam or Eve. It is strange, but the only time they reference themselves in the plural is before their fall into sin. Eve says, "*We* may eat of the fruit of the trees in the garden" (v. 2, emphasis added). After that, it is all singular. When Eve gives birth to Cain, she says, "*I* have gotten a man with the help of the Lord" (4:1, emphasis added). When Eve gives birth to Seth, she says, "God has appointed for *me* another offspring instead of Abel, for Cain killed him" (v. 25, emphasis added).

Make of this what you will, but not until the birth of Noah does the Bible again record a human using the first-person plural. Noah's father, Lamech, says, "Out of the ground that the Lord has cursed, this one shall bring *us* relief from *our* work and from the painful toil of *our* hands" (5:29, emphasis added).

Adam is incomplete without Eve. He is not whole until she is created. Yes, God makes a good creation, but God Himself says, "It is not good that the man should be *alone*" (2:18, emphasis added). It is not good for us to be alone, to be isolated. Community is good. Fellowship is good. Friendship is good.

Satan drives a wedge between Adam and Eve that isolates them from each other. Now, I'm not saying that Adam and Eve never referred to themselves as "we/our/us" for the rest of their lives. But there is something striking about the Scriptures not recording such togetherness after the fall. Adam and Eve brought forth an isolation and a cursed ground that are not transformed until the days of Noah.

SATAN'S DESIRED OUTCOME

Peter writes, "Your adversary the devil prowls around like a roaring lion, seeking someone to devour" (1 Peter 5:8). If you have ever watched a nature show that featured lions or most any cat, you have likely seen their strategy for hunting. They locate a vulnerable victim and then isolate it.

Peter's comparison of Satan to a lion is most apt. Satan loves this lie because he knows that God's people are more easily devoured when they are alone. Satan loves this lie because it works.

> *Satan desires that we are isolated from other Christians. Satan wants us to be separated from the Body of Christ.*

Satan's desired outcome is for us to internalize this lie, to repeat it to ourselves again and again: "I am alone. I am alone." As we internalize and repeat the lie, we are in danger of making the lie a reality and isolating ourselves.

Satan desires that we are isolated from other Christians. Satan wants us to be separated from the Body of Christ. Satan wants us distant from family and friends, fellowship and community. He wants us to shun those things.

Satan also desires that we are as distant from God as possible, that we are disconnected from God's promises. Satan does not want us to hear God's Word, receive God's forgiveness, participate in the Lord's Supper, or sing God's praises.

Yet choosing to gather with other people does not make us immune to this lie. Satan also knows this counterintuitive truth: we often feel most alone in a crowd of people. As we look around the room and see others conversing easily, laughing, and enjoying themselves, a feeling like we do not belong can seep into our hearts. We feel as David did when he wrote, "Look to the right and see: there is none who takes notice of me; no refuge remains to me; no one cares for my soul" (Psalm 142:4).

Sometimes, the more people there are around us, the more alone we feel and the more we notice the connections we lack but others seem to have.

Whether we are physically alone or lost in a crowd, Satan desires that we feel isolated. Once we feel alone, he nudges us in various directions. Satan might push us toward self-loathing: "I'm alone because I'm unlovable." "Nobody notices me because I'm worthless." And Satan never misses an opportunity to push us toward hating others, so he also wants us to think, "Nobody notices me because they are all jerks," or, "I'm alone because all my friends forgot me and actually hate me."

Hating others and loathing ourselves will bring us further and further from the community we so desperately need and were created to participate in.

But Satan can also move us in another more subtle direction: feeling self-assured in being alone. Satan persuades us to be alone as the path of least resistance. The lie becomes "You are alone, and it is easier and better that way."

When relationships with family, friends, or fellow Christians are difficult and complicated, Satan prompts us to consider how much easier and simpler life would be without those relationships. This is challenging because it may very well be true. And there are times when relationships are abusive and harmful and should end.

> *When relationships with family, friends, or fellow Christians are difficult and complicated, Satan prompts us to consider how much easier and simpler life would be without those relationships.*

But Satan does not want us separated from abusive and harmful relationships. He wants us stuck in those relationships with no way out. Satan wants us separated from relationships that are merely challenging and require patience. Satan despises love and joy. He wants us removed from relationships where love, joy, and patience are possible and present and instead imprisoned where hate and misery abound.

THE FEAR BEHIND THE LIE

On the surface, this lie and the fear behind it are one and the same. "You are alone" preys on the fear of being alone.

But the fear of being alone is not simply a matter of loneliness. Being truly alone means being without security, without any support, help, or guidance—these are much deeper fears.

This interplays with the previous lie: "If I am alone and without support, then I will have to take care of and save myself." Such fears lead us either to a place of uncertainty, where we lack assurance, or to a place where we find assurance in ourselves.

As we lack assurance, we constantly question those around us, including God, and are filled with worry that we have been abandoned. This may lead us to wonder why and push us toward Lie 7 (that God does not love us) or Lie 10 (that we are too flawed to be loved).

These fears fuse together in dreadful chaos. And we are always more susceptible to them when we are disconnected from God, His promises, and His people. The fear that we are without security and support may lead us to distrust others. If we look to a friend for support and they do not provide it, we will begin to distrust them. We may not look to them for support in the future. We may turn to another friend for support instead or simply move forward on our own.

Often, before we choose to reach out for support from others, Satan seizes the opportunity to lead us into fear. It takes only one example of imperfect support for Satan to tell us that we are alone. That nobody can be trusted. That nobody will support us. Turning to another friend is not the answer because they will fail us too—everyone will.

Satan uses every failure of friendship and family and church relationships to push this lie and this fear on us, that we are alone. And Satan also uses such failures of relationship to lead us toward self-reliance. Satan backs us into resignation: "Yeah, you are alone, but that is totally fine. Better even. It's just easier this way."

THE LIE REPEATED IN THE BIBLE

ELIJAH

After Elijah defeats the prophets of Baal in 1 Kings 18:20–40, he receives a message from Queen Jezebel, saying she is going to kill him. So Elijah runs for his life. He runs for over a hundred miles. And when he gets to Beersheba, the southern border of ancient Israel, he stops. He goes off alone into the wilderness and tells God to take his life.

One thing about this story that often gets overlooked is that Elijah does not make the hundred-mile run for his life alone. He has a servant with him the whole time. It is not until he reaches Beersheba that Elijah sends the servant away. All this happens in the span of one verse: "Then [Elijah] was afraid, and he arose and ran for his life and came to Beersheba, which belongs to Judah, and left his servant there" (1 Kings 19:3).

We know almost nothing about this servant. But Elijah's action of sending the servant away is something many of us are prone to do. When we feel lonely, we push others away. When we feel like no one cares, we shove away anybody who might try to care. When we feel like we are completely on our own, we manifest that fear and make it come to pass.

But Elijah does not die in the wilderness of Beersheba. The angel of the Lord comes and feeds Elijah with miraculous bread and water, strengthening him for the journey ahead. Where does Elijah choose to go? Out of Israel, down to Mount Sinai, also known as Mount Horeb. This is the place where God

> *When we feel like no one cares, we shove away anybody who might try to care.*

spoke to Moses face to face, so Elijah is headed there to tell God the lie that he has believed: "I, even I only, am left" (v. 10). I am alone.

167

But Elijah is not alone. He has never been alone. There are prophets hiding in caves that he was told about and ignored (see 1 Kings 18:13). The Israelites have repented and left behind the idols of Baal and Asherah, as 1 Kings 18:17–40 tells us. And then, of course, there is the servant whom Elijah left in Beersheba (1Kings 19:3) and the widow and her son whom Elijah stayed with (1 Kings 17:8–16). And even more people whom Elijah does not yet know about but soon will.

God tells Elijah that he is not alone. There is a community waiting for him—seven thousand people preserved and reserved who have never bowed down to the false god Baal. God sends Elijah back with work to do, but He makes sure someone is with Elijah for the rest of his days: another prophet, named Elisha.

It is interesting that at the end of Elijah's time on earth, he seeks to be alone once more. Before Elijah's exit from the world, he tries three times to send Elisha away (see 2 Kings 2:1–12). But Elisha stays close and watches his mentor go up into the heavens in a whirlwind. Elijah was not alone.

NAOMI

At the beginning of the book of Ruth, everything has gone wrong for Naomi. A famine hits, so she and her husband, Elimelech, and their two sons leave their home in Bethlehem to sojourn in Moab. While there, their two sons get married to Moabite women. But Elimelech dies. Then the two sons die. Naomi is bereft. She is in a foreign land completely vulnerable without a penny to her name, with two daughters-in-law in tow. Naomi was without support, without security, without help, without guidance. She hears that the famine is over in Judah, so she seeks to return to Bethlehem.

Naomi wants to make this journey alone. She seeks to send her daughters-in-law back to their families. One daughter-in-law, Orpah, agrees to go back to her Moabite family. But the other, Ruth, refuses. Ruth stubbornly will not let Naomi go alone. So they go together.

Sometimes grief and loss make us feel terribly alone. Naomi had lost her husband and her two sons. If you were to lose three family members in quick succession, you, too, would probably think with great frequency, "I am so alone." The loss of one person can make life feel horribly unstable and uncertain. The loss of several loved ones can make us want to huddle in a corner and hide alone. Feeling alone has a way of making us seek out more loneliness.

When Naomi returns with Ruth to Bethlehem, people ask, "Is this Naomi?" (Ruth 1:19). Naomi responds,

> **Do not call me Naomi; call me Mara, for the Almighty has dealt very bitterly with me. I went away full, and the LORD has brought me back empty. Why call me Naomi, when the LORD has testified against me and the Almighty has brought calamity upon me? (vv. 21–22)**

Naomi's name means "pleasant." The name she chooses for herself, *Mara*, means "bitter."

Ruth goes out to glean grain from a field. She happens on a field owned by Boaz, a relative of Elimelech, Ruth's deceased father-in-law. Boaz shows Ruth and Naomi kindness. Despite all the tragedy, when opportunity comes, when Naomi hears of Boaz's care, she immediately responds with faithfulness, "May he be blessed by the LORD, whose kindness has not forsaken the living or the dead!" (2:20).

God restores the fortunes of Naomi and Ruth. Ruth and Boaz get married. Their security is restored. The book ends with Naomi caring for a grandchild. Naomi was not alone.

THE WOMAN AT THE WELL

In John 4, Jesus and His disciples enter a Samaritan village called Sychar. After Jesus sends His disciples away to find some food, He stays and rests at a well. Around noon, a Samaritan woman comes to draw water from the well. This would not have been the customary time to draw water. Most people would have gone early in the morning or in the evening to avoid carrying heavy water vessels in the heat of the day.

The Samaritan woman's choice to draw water at noon signals that perhaps she does not want to be around other people. After her conversation with Jesus, it becomes clear that this woman has had a difficult life. She has had five husbands. No matter how those marriages came to an end, it cannot have been an easy road. Divorce was not something women could initiate in that culture. This woman has either been widowed or abandoned and sent away by five husbands.

I do not know, but I wonder if this woman felt like being alone was just easier. I wonder if she found herself not wanting to be at the well with other people in her community because it was just difficult and annoying. Maybe people made thoughtless or passive-aggressive comments about her. Maybe they felt pity for her. Maybe they kept their distance.

Whatever the case, she comes to the well alone, seemingly expecting to do her chore alone, and she encounters Jesus. Jesus reveals to her that He is the long-awaited Messiah. Jesus' presence, words, and revelation prompt this woman to go to her community and invite the people there to come and see Jesus. Jesus stays in their village for two days, and the people make a wondrous confession, saying of Jesus, "We know that this is indeed the Savior of the world" (John 4:42).

Jesus brings about faith in this community through a woman who was in danger of being excluded and excluding herself from the community.

THE LIE REPEATED IN OUR WORLD

In our world, one of the places where this lie becomes most apparent is social media. How many times have you seen a guilt trip post that goes something like "Most people won't like this, but if you actually care about me, I know you will." Or "Most people will ignore this, but if you really love Jesus, comment 'Amen.'"

I cannot tell you how many times I have shared a piece I have written and just waited for the notifications to pour in with all the likes and shares I will get. In my head, I estimate how many each post will get, and I am disappointed even if the number far surpasses my expectations. If I get ten likes, I want twenty. If I get twenty, I want fifty. If I get fifty, I want a hundred. If I get a hundred, I want a thousand. There is no quenching my thirst for likes and shares and comments and retweets (or whatever we are calling those now).

And whenever I do not get enough, according to my made-up standard, I feel alone. I just shared a blog post twenty-two minutes ago. And nobody has liked it yet. And Satan is lying to me at this very minute, telling me that I am alone. Telling me that nobody cares what I have to say. Telling me that I should stop writing this book. "If nobody cares about a blog post, why would they care about a book? Don't give away all your energy to a project that nobody will read."

I do not know how many copies this book will sell, but I guarantee it will never be enough for me not to be vulnerable to Satan's favorite lie in my life that I am alone.

It is insidious because it is so obviously not true. I do not need to think terribly hard to list off dozens of people who love me, and yet when their names come to mind, Satan has some accusation lined up for each one of them that questions if they truly do love me. Satan raises doubts over every relationship and ultimately brings me back to the first lie—that I cannot trust even my relationship with God.

I am like a sheep that has twisted its ankle. Satan, the prowling lion, nips at my heels, making me panic. I turn left, then right, then completely away from my community of safety and love until I am, in fact, alone, isolated from others. And in my isolation, Satan begins to feast on my despair and hopelessness.

Until along comes Jesus. He comes looking for me, the lost sheep.

Until along comes Jesus. He comes looking for me, the lost sheep. He smacks that lion Satan in the face with His shepherd's staff, and He lifts me up out of the mess and brings me back to the flock, my community, His people.

Jesus knows the lion will return. He knows that I will get isolated again. He knows that He will have to come looking for me again, probably tomorrow, maybe later today. Yet He still comes and finds me when I am most alone, and He is present with me.

THE TRUTH

The truth is that we are not alone. When Jesus' birth is revealed to Joseph, we are told, "All this took place to fulfill what the Lord had spoken by the prophet: 'Behold, the virgin shall conceive and bear a son, and they shall call His name Immanuel' (which means, God with us)" (Matthew 1:22–23). God is with us.

When Adam and Eve fall into sin, God does not abandon them to be alone. He comes looking for them. The first words out of God's mouth after the fall are "Where are you?" (Genesis 3:9).

I find it interesting that in the parable Jesus tells about the lost sheep, only one sheep is lost. It is not a few that have lost their way but at least have one another. It is one. One that is alone. The truth is that Jesus goes out and finds that one lost sheep. Yes, He finds it because it is lost and He desires it found, but He also brings it back to the other ninety-nine. Jesus desires that this sheep is not alone.

Jesus is your Good Shepherd. He goes out and finds you when you are lost and alone. He will bring you back to the flock, to the green pastures and still waters, to the table prepared and overflowing with good things.

After His resurrection but before His ascension, Jesus promises His disciples, "Behold, I am with you always, to the end of the age" (Matthew 28:20).

The Scriptures are filled with promises of God's presence. You are not alone.

GOD'S DESIRED OUTCOME

God's desired outcome is that we always remember His presence, that we are surrounded by a community of faithful people who will support us and help us. God wants us to be surrounded by a great cloud of witnesses both here on earth and into eternity.

While Satan drives us to isolate, Jesus seeks us. Jesus is with us. Jesus brings us into community. While Satan prowls like a roaring lion, Jesus defends us as our Good Shepherd.

God sees to His desired outcome again and again in the Old Testament, being present with His people to bring them out of Egypt, to guide them through the wilderness, and to lead them into the Promised Land. God's presence is with His people. Then, in the incarnation of Jesus, God's presence takes a new form. And in the return of Jesus, God's presence will enter its final and ultimate setting, for we will always be with the Lord in the new creation and everlasting life.

As John writes,

> And I heard a loud voice from the throne saying,
> "Behold, the dwelling place of God is with man. He
> will dwell with them, and they will be His people,
> and God Himself will be with them as their God. He
> will wipe away every tear from their eyes, and death

shall be no more, neither shall there be mourning, nor crying, nor pain anymore, for the former things have passed away." (Revelation 21:3–4)

THE LOVE THAT CASTS OUT FEAR

In Psalm 107, the poet begins by writing, "Oh give thanks to the LORD, for He is good, for His steadfast love endures forever!" (v. 1). The author then proceeds to list out examples of God's love, situations where God shows up and delivers people.

Perhaps the most interesting of these is this:

Some wandered in desert wastes, finding no way to a city to dwell in; hungry and thirsty, their soul fainted within them. Then they cried to the LORD in their trouble, and He delivered them from their distress. He led them by a straight way till they reached a city to dwell in. (Psalm 107:4–7)

Those who are wandering need to be shown the way. That makes sense. Yet one might presume the path would go to a different location. At least to my mind, those who are wandering in the desert need to be shown the way to water, to a river, a lake, an oasis, a stream. But that is not where the path goes. It goes to a city. The way out of the desert leads to a place to live, a community to dwell in.

> *When we are wandering alone and in need, God shows us the way to a city to dwell in.*

When we are wandering alone and in need, God shows us the way to a city to dwell in. Indeed, God sends Jesus to be the way to the eternal city, the new Jerusalem. In that eternal city, which Jesus has gone to prepare for us, we will never be alone. We will never fear the possibility of being without support or without help. We will be with all the faithful whose robes have been washed by the blood of Jesus. And more than that, as Paul says: "And so we will always be with the Lord" (1 Thessalonians 4:17).

Questions for Reflection

Where do you see this lie appearing in your life?

In what situations do you find yourself
isolating from others?

Can you remember a time when you were afraid of being
without support? What was that like?

Whom can you trust to tell you the truth when you are
struggling with this lie?

Can you think of other biblical characters who struggled
with loneliness?

Scripture for Meditation

Psalm 121

Joshua 1:1–9

Zephaniah 3:14–20

Matthew 1:18–25

LIE 10

YOU ARE TOO DIRTY/ BROKEN/ FLAWED/ SINFUL TO BE FORGIVEN

I grew up on a farm. If you walked out of our front door and took a left, you would immediately cross a dirt and gravel driveway that led to one of our fields. On the other side of the driveway there was a crabapple tree and a long hose attached to a water spigot. My grand-ma's garden was close by, and she needed the hose to stretch to her flowers and vegetables.

In the summertime, my brothers and I would play for hours and hours outside. One of the games that got us into the most trouble was what we called "mudman." We would flood the dirt and gravel drive-way, make mud, and spread the mud all over ourselves. The one time I can remember going into the house covered in mud, I was immedi-ately escorted back outside. I was too dirty to be welcomed inside. I needed to clean off first. I needed to wash the mud away.

> *Satan wants us to believe that we are too covered in filth to be welcomed into the house of God.*

Satan wants us to believe that we are too covered in filth to be welcomed into the house of God, that our brokenness is too much for God to heal, that we have to clean ourselves up first. With every lie Satan tells, he heaps reminders of our sin on us, pointing us forward to this final lie, that there is some-thing so wrong with us that we cannot be forgiven, that we cannot be welcomed by God's grace.

SATAN IN THE GARDEN

The inception of this lie is perhaps the most difficult to pinpoint. In part, this is because the dialogue between Satan and Eve is cut off once the fall into sin occurs. We do not hear what Satan has to say to Adam and Eve once they fall into sin and become flawed.

Two clues are disclosed that this lie has taken root in Adam and Eve: first, that they hide themselves and, second, that they seek to clothe themselves. As they internalize Lie 6—that they must cover up their sins—they simultaneously cover up themselves. They are their sin. This internalization of sin as our very identity is something Satan still seeks to accomplish in each of us today.

Adam and Eve's choice to sew fig leaves for themselves is a choice not merely to cover their sin but also to cover themselves, to cover their shame, to cover their dirty, broken, flawed existence. Our propensity to hide and cover not just our sin but our very selves is an indication that we are being assaulted by this lie.

When God comes down to find Adam and Eve, one thing Adam says is "I was afraid, because I was naked, and I hid myself" (Genesis 3:10). God's question to Adam is "Who told you that you were naked?" (v. 11).

Adam and Eve are naked and afraid of God, so they cover up and hide from Him. They know they have disobeyed, and they are ashamed. They are terrified of the consequences of their disobedience. Whatever happened to their minds and souls and bodies and all of creation in the fall, it included this lie running through their minds: you are too dirty/broken/flawed to be forgiven, so be afraid and hide.

SATAN'S DESIRED OUTCOME

Satan's desired outcome with this lie is exactly what we see from Adam and Eve: that we would be ashamed and hide from God. Satan desires that we would run as far away from God as possible. In our fear that we are too flawed to be forgiven, Satan wants us to run as far away from forgiveness and the Forgiver as possible.

Satan loves this lie because, in speaking it, he convinces us to put aside the armor God has given us to see what lies beneath. Satan persuades us to tear up the perfect clothing of Christ, the robe of His righteousness, to gaze at our mangled, sinful flesh. Satan wants us to ignore what God has done to cleanse and clothe us, heal and restore us. Satan wants us to rewind our lives and pause on all the worst moments, looking back at all the sin and shame and failure in our past.

Satan holds up those images where we are at our worst as often as possible and tries to persuade us that this is who we are and nothing can change it.

> *Satan persuades us to tear up the perfect clothing of Christ, the robe of His righteousness, to gaze at our mangled, sinful flesh.*

Any time Satan reminds you of that one big sin in your past, this is the lie he is telling you. He whispers or shouts, "Don't you remember what you did? You are not clean. Just look at this thing. Look at it! God cannot accept you after that."

Or sometimes Satan will go for a cumulative angle. "How long have you been struggling with this sin? It's been decades! It might be small, but over time, this adds up to a debt you simply cannot pay. And there is no sign of you stopping this sin, is there? You are too flawed to be forgiven."

Satan also loves this lie because it does not even need to involve our own sin. Sometimes we feel dirty and broken and flawed because of sin that has been done to us. Those who have been abused often hear this lie, not only from Satan but also from society. Sadly, we also frequently hear this lie from the church. How often are people blamed for violence done to them? How common is it for a woman to be implicitly blamed for being sexually assaulted? Awful questions arise, like, "Well, what was she wearing?"

How often are particular sins called out with such force in our congregations or at our dinner tables that anyone who might have been associated with such sins feels like there is no hope for them, no place for them? How many deaths by suicide have been caused by this lie?

Satan's desired outcome is for people to give up on the very idea of forgiveness for themselves and for others. Satan wants us to view God and His people as pernicious, unforgiving, and cruel.

But moreover, Satan's desired outcome is for the church to be just that: unforgiving and cruel. Satan wants the church to repeat this lie to God's people, to hold forward an unbearable standard that we force on others but refuse to carry ourselves.

Satan does not just want us repeating this lie to ourselves. He wants us repeating this lie to one another. He wants this lie to be the mantra of every church and every Christian throughout the world. Satan wants us to be evangelists of unforgiveness.

THE FEAR BEHIND THE LIE

Once again, the lie and the fear behind it are the same. We all know that we are not perfect. We each make mistakes. Sin is a part of our lives yesterday, today, and tomorrow. We fear that our sin and flaws are too much for God to handle, too much for God to overlook, too much for God to forgive.

Each of Satan's lies points back toward the first lie that we cannot trust God, but each lie also leans us forward toward the despair of this lie that we are beyond forgiveness.

Consider how this plays out with the previous lies. Satan lies to you and tells you that you deserve more, so you take more. But then you feel guilty. You realize your mistake, and you repent, seeking God's forgiveness. But then Satan picks up your sin again and shoves it in your face and says, "No, no, no. You took way more than you should have. This example of sin is too bad, too heavy, too egregious to be forgiven." This is a lie.

Or perhaps Satan lies by telling you that you need to seize control of a situation, so you do. Your actions cause lots of damage to other people, needlessly hurting them by your desire for control. And when they bring it to your attention, you double down and seize even more control. You force people to resign. You manipulate others to help you oust all the nay-sayers. Pretty soon everything begins to crumble around you, and you are faced with the reality that you have believed a lie. You confess. You repent. You seek forgiveness from God and those you have harmed, but Satan is ready. All he has to do is show you the mess you have made and say, "You caused all this. And you expect forgiveness? God might be slow to anger, but He is not that slow." This is a lie.

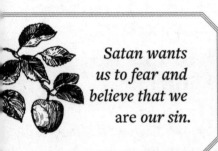

Satan wants us to fear and believe that we are our sin.

The more Satan does this, the less we are able to delineate between what we do and who we are. Soon we begin to hear Satan say, "How many times do you think God is going to forgive you for this? If you cannot stop this sin, then clearly you are damaged beyond repair. Clearly something is wrong with you. You are a bad batch. You are too flawed to be forgiven."

Satan wants us to fear that we cannot be forgiven. Moreover, Satan wants us to fear and believe that we *are* our sin, that each sin we commit cannot be removed from who we are.

THE LIE REPEATED IN THE BIBLE

JOSHUA THE HIGH PRIEST

One of the more obscure passages where Satan is mentioned begins in Zechariah 3:1: "Then he showed me Joshua the high priest standing before the angel of the LORD, and Satan standing at his right hand to accuse him." Zechariah sees a vision of Joshua the high priest standing before the angel of the Lord. Satan stands by, doing what Satan does: accusing God's people. Zechariah describes Joshua the high priest as "clothed with filthy garments" (v. 3).

But God rebukes Satan for his accusations of Joshua. Then the angel of the Lord says to remove Joshua's filthy garments and tells Joshua, "Behold, I have taken your iniquity away from you, and I will clothe you with pure vestments" (v. 4).

We are not told what accusations Satan is bringing against Joshua the high priest. All we are told is that Joshua is clothed in these filthy garments. The scene moves on quickly (and we will examine the truths laid forth in Zechariah 3 below), but I see a connection between Joshua's filthy garments and his sin. We see Joshua reclothed in pure vestments, which connects to forgiveness.

Other biblical authors make a similar connection. Isaiah writes, "We have all become like one who is unclean, and all our righteous deeds are like a polluted garment. We all fade like a leaf, and our iniquities, like the wind, take us away" (Isaiah 64:6).

Filthy clothing is an indication of sinfulness. Pure vestments, washed robes, are an indication of forgiveness.

As Satan stands accusing Joshua the high priest, I imagine Satan saying, "Look at you. You are covered in filth. You are far too dirty to be in God's presence. How dare you even show your face here. What further witnesses do we need?" We will see the end of the story below, when we get to the truth.

JONAH

God calls the prophet Jonah, saying, "Arise, go to Nineveh, that great city, and call out against it, for their evil has come up before Me" (Jonah 1:2). Jonah says, "I don't think so," and runs the other direction. God stops Jonah's detour, and Jonah finds himself swallowed by a fish and then vomited on shore with the same call to go and prophesy against Nineveh. When Jonah arrives at Nineveh, he says, "Yet forty days, and Nineveh shall be overthrown!" (3:4). It is a pretty short sermon, but it proves effective, as all the inhabitants of the city repent in sackcloth and ashes.

God then relents from disaster. Nineveh is not overthrown by devastation as we might have expected. Nineveh is overturned in a different way. The people repent of their evil and are transformed.

Yet this is exactly what Jonah expected. And Jonah is infuriated by Nineveh's repentance and God's relenting from disaster. In his anger, he prays to the Lord and says,

> O LORD, is not this what I said when I was yet in my country? That is why I made haste to flee to Tarshish; for I knew that You are a gracious God and merciful, slow to anger and abounding in steadfast love, and relenting from disaster. Therefore now, O LORD, please take my life from me, for it is better for me to die than to live. (4:2–3)

Jonah wants Nineveh to be blasted from the face of the earth. Jonah does not want God's grace to come to the people of Nineveh. Jonah's plan was to run away and not provide the Lord's warning. If the people were not warned, they would not repent and God would annihilate them, which is exactly what Jonah wanted: his enemies destroyed.

> *God shows Jonah His way of mercy and grace. Even the people of Nineveh, with all their great evil, are not beyond forgiveness.*

Jonah believed this lie about the people of Nineveh, that they were too flawed to be forgiven. Jonah wanted nothing more than for that lie to become the truth. But God shows Jonah His way of mercy and grace. Even the people of Nineveh, with all their great evil, are not beyond forgiveness.

THE LIE REPEATED IN OUR WORLD

Like Jonah, we believe this lie about other people. To us, some sins are simply past the point of forgiveness. We give up on such people and relationships. We write them off and pray for their demise, and Satan cheers us along every step of the way.

We forget that Jesus calls on us to love our enemies. We forget that God does not delight in obliterating evil people. He Himself says, "As I live, declares the LORD GOD, I have no pleasure in the death of the wicked, but that the wicked turn from his way and live" (Ezekiel 33:11).

Likewise, as Jesus says, "Just so, I tell you, there will be more joy in heaven over one sinner who repents than over ninety-nine righteous persons who need no repentance" (Luke 15:7).

We should never delight in the death of anyone. We should never believe or hope that any sinner is beyond repentance.

It is dangerous to believe this lie about others, but in our world, we also swallow and repeat this lie about ourselves.

I find this lie relates to Lie 5. As Satan consistently turns our attention toward our sinfulness, rubbing our faces in it, he wants us to plug our ears to the call of repentance and forgiveness. Satan wants us to believe that we have out-sinned God's grace, that the forgiveness we hear about is something we are exempt from because our sin is too great, our flaws too numerous, our filth too disgusting even for a gracious God. Satan is a liar.

One of the ways I have seen this take place involves a deep fear of the so-called unforgivable sin. Jesus says,

> **Every sin and blasphemy will be forgiven people, but the blasphemy against the Spirit will not be forgiven. And whoever speaks a word against the Son of Man will be forgiven, but whoever speaks against the Holy Spirit will not be forgiven, either in this age or in the age to come. (Matthew 12:31–32)**

Jesus says this blasphemy against the Holy Spirit will not be forgiven. I have encountered several people over the years who are paralyzed by the thought that they have committed this sin and now are beyond forgiveness.

This is not easy to address in writing. It is a topic much better dealt with in conversation. But I will point those in fear to the context surrounding Jesus' words. Jesus has just cast out a demon. The religious leaders of the day accuse Jesus of using the powers of Beelzebul to cast out the demon. This is not the case. Jesus points out their flawed logic. Jesus is filled with the Holy Spirit. It is by the Spirit that demonic forces are cast out. These religious leaders are accusing Jesus of using witchcraft and consorting with demonic powers. Thus they are accusing the Holy Spirit of being demonic.

Those who actually blaspheme the Holy Spirit would never fear doing so. Moreover, they would never flee to the Holy Spirit for forgiveness. If you are afraid you have blasphemed the Holy Spirit, the very reality that you seek forgiveness tells me you have not committed this sin. You are forgivable because the power of Jesus' blood is greater than any and all of your sins.

> *You are forgivable because the power of Jesus' blood is greater than any and all of your sins.*

Luther wrote letters to many people who were in spiritual distress, who were enduring the assaults and lies of the devil. One common spiritual distress Luther addresses in his letters is uncertainty over eternal election—in other words, when someone is struggling to believe that they are indeed saved by Christ. Luther frequently points people in such distress to look to Jesus. Luther invites them to turn to Jesus in prayer, turn to Jesus and His words of eternal life.

If you, as you are reading this, fear that you are not saved, that you are past forgiveness, look to Jesus. He is the perfecter of your faith. And when you struggle with doubts and disbelief, pray the prayer of the distressed father with a demon-possessed son in Mark 9:24: "I believe; help my unbelief."

THE TRUTH

To reveal the truth, let us return to our earlier example from the book of Zechariah. Zechariah (much like the books of Daniel, Ezekiel, Revelation, and parts of Isaiah) is a prophetic book of apocalyptic literature. It is a bit strange to read when we do not have a modern-day equivalent of this genre of literature. There are a lot of images and numbers in these books that sound quite strange. But as we read through this section of Zechariah 3, we hear three things clearly.

First, God rebukes Satan and Satan's accusations. He tells Satan, "The LORD rebuke you, O Satan! The LORD who has chosen Jerusalem rebuke you!" (Zechariah 3:2).

Second, Joshua the high priest is cleansed and given clean clothes instead of his filthy rags, as we noted before.

Third, God promises the forgiveness of His people in a single day, through the one He calls "My servant the Branch" (v. 8). We now know how God brought this about: by Jesus' death and resurrection. Jesus is the promised Branch who takes away the iniquity of the world. Satan's accusations have no place anymore. God has rebuked Satan and turned his accusations into lies. We are no longer clothed in filthy rags; we are clothed with the pure robe of Christ's righteousness.

You are not too dirty to be cleansed. You are not too broken to be healed. You are not too flawed to be perfected. You are not too sinful to be forgiven. You are cleansed, healed, perfected, forgiven by Jesus.

The truth is that no one is too dirty/broken/flawed/sinful to be forgiven. Consider the people God calls into His service. Think about some of the people in Hebrews 11, a chapter on faithfulness. Noah was a drunkard. Abraham was a liar. Sarah laughed at God. Isaac was a liar just like his father. Jacob was a master of deception. Joseph was arrogant and pompous. Moses was a murderer. The people of Israel might have crossed the Red Sea in faith, but that generation all died in the wilderness because they constantly grumbled against God and distrusted Him. The people of Israel may have entered the Promised Land and brought Jericho down, but they failed to possess the land as God had instructed them to do, because they were afraid.

> *You are not too dirty to be cleansed. You are not too broken to be healed. You are not too flawed to be perfected. You are not too sinful to be forgiven.*

Rahab was a prostitute. Gideon was a coward. Barak was a coward. Samson was terribly problematic. Jephthah murdered his own daughter because of an idiotic vow. David was a murderer. Samuel raised sons who turned out to be just as treacherous as his master Eli's sons.

Or we could talk about the people of the New Testament whom Jesus calls to follow Him. Peter denied Jesus and tried to stop Jesus from dying and rising. James and John presumptively wanted to sit at Jesus' right and left in His glory. Thomas disbelieved Jesus was risen. Matthew was a tax collector. Paul put Stephen to death and persecuted the church. Mark abandoned the mission of Paul and Barnabas. Jesus' own mother and brothers (including James) wanted Jesus to stop teaching.

God calls all these people, in all their flaws and brokenness, to follow Him and be His servants. These are the great cloud of witnesses that surround us. And we do not set our eyes on them, but we fix our eyes on Jesus, "the founder and perfecter of our faith" (Hebrews 12:2). Or, as I like to say, the author and editor of our faith.

No matter who you are or what you have done or what has been done to you, no flaw is beyond God's re-creation. No sin beyond God's forgiveness. No brokenness beyond His healing. No dirt that cannot be cleansed by the blood of Christ.

GOD'S DESIRED OUTCOME

God's desired outcome is one that He brings about Himself. He clothes you in righteousness. He washes your robes in the blood of Jesus. Now, God wants us to get used to living in those pure vestments, for they will be our eternal clothing. God wants us to stop peeking under our robes of righteousness to see how dirty we are underneath. God wants us to stop viewing our filth and sin as the real us and start viewing ourselves as He sees us—His cleansed, restored, perfect children.

God knows that we will remain sinful until we die or Jesus returns, whichever comes first. But out of His deep love for us, God forgives our sin through Jesus. God wants us to leave our sin behind at the foot of Jesus' cross and live under Him in His kingdom.

In Psalm 25:6–7, David prays,

> Remember Your mercy, O LORD, and Your steadfast love, for they have been from of old. Remember not the sins of my youth or my transgressions; according to Your steadfast love remember me, for the sake of Your goodness, O LORD!

God's love remembers our sin no more. His desired outcome is just that. Now He invites us to forget our forgiven sin, to leave it at the foot of the cross and follow Him.

God does not overlook our sin.
God removes our sin.

191

THE LOVE THAT CASTS OUT FEAR

We fear that our sin is too great for God to overlook. God does not overlook our sin. God removes our sin. In Psalm 103:10–12, this is what David writes regarding how God handles our sin:

> **He does not deal with us according to our sins, nor repay us according to our iniquities. For as high as the heavens are above the earth, so great is His steadfast love toward those who fear Him; as far as the east is from the west, so far does He remove our transgressions from us.**

As high as the heavens are above the earth, that is how far God has removed your sin from you through Jesus' death. The farthest star away from us that astronomers have observed with the James Webb Telescope is 28 billion light years away. It is called Earendel. If we wanted to get there, we would have to travel at the speed of light—186,000 miles per second—for 28 billion years. Earendel is the highest thing we can see in the sky, in the heavens.

Imagine God taking your sins and removing them 28 billion light years away from you. They would have no chance of ever touching you again. They would be too far away.

God has removed them even further away from you than that in the space of Jesus' outstretched arms on the cross. Your sin is removed. Forgiven. Gone. You need not fear that you are too sinful to be forgiven, for God's love removes your sin further away from you than you can fathom.

Questions for Reflection

Where do you see this lie appearing in your life?

What sins do you find it hard to believe Jesus has forgiven?

Can you remember a time when you were afraid that you were broken beyond repair? What was that like?

Whom can you trust to tell you the truth when you are struggling with this lie?

Can you think of other biblical characters who believed they were beyond forgiveness?

Scripture for Meditation

Psalm 51

Isaiah 53

Hebrews 9:11–28

Mark 2:1–12

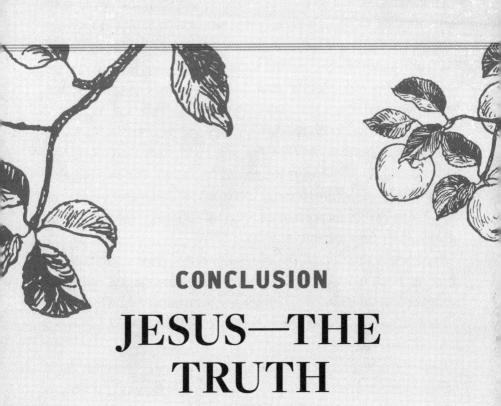

CONCLUSION

JESUS—THE TRUTH

Jesus is real. He has been crucified and is risen for you and your salvation. Jesus is safe. Jesus is dedicated to dismantling Satan's evil actions. One of Jesus' primary tactics in the war against Satan is quite simple: the truth. Satan is a liar and the father of lies. Jesus is the truth. He says, "I am the way, and the truth, and the life. No one comes to the Father except through Me" (John 14:6).

Where Satan strives to obscure our way and separate us from God and His love, Jesus draws near, not only by bringing God's love with Him, not only by showing us the way to God's love, but also by being God's love to us. Satan seeks our destruction. Jesus seeks our salvation. Satan wishes us present and eternal suffering. Jesus brings us abundant life now and into eternity.

Jesus seeks to undo all the evil Satan does. Where Satan plants discord, Jesus makes unity blossom. Where Satan grows pride and arrogance, Jesus overflows such gardens with humility and meekness. Where Satan spreads darkness, Jesus shines light. Where Satan lies, Jesus stands ready with truth.

Toward the beginning of his Gospel, John writes, "And the Word became flesh and dwelt among us, and we have seen His glory, glory as of the only Son from the Father, full of grace and truth" (John 1:14). Jesus is the Word. Jesus is full of grace and full of truth.

Jesus, full of grace and truth, is the inception of all goodness. He is at the center of humanity's salvation from sin and death. He leads us from death to life, from sin to forgiveness. He saves us from Satan and all of Satan's lies.

When Jesus is on trial before Pontius Pilate, Jesus says, "You say that I am a king. For this purpose I was born and for this purpose I have come into the world—to bear witness to the truth. Everyone who is of the truth listens to My voice" (John 18:37). Pilate responds with a question: "What is truth?" (v. 38). Pilate's question is not answered, but we know the answer. Jesus Himself is the truth.

Jesus is the truth. He is described as the true light (John 1:9), as true food and true drink (6:55), as the true vine (15:1), and as the true witness (Revelation 3:14). John also writes, "And we know that the Son of God has come and has given us understanding, so that we may know Him who is true; and we are in Him who is true, in His Son Jesus Christ. He is the true God and eternal life" (1 John 5:20).

Since Jesus is the truth, everything He says is true. Everything He says about Himself is true. Everything He says about you is true as well. Here are some of the promises Jesus speaks to His followers.

"You are the light of the world" (Matthew 5:14).

"You are the salt of the earth" (Matthew 5:13).

"Come to Me, all who labor and are heavy laden, and I will give you rest. Take My yoke upon you, and learn from Me, for I am gentle and lowly in heart, and you will find rest for your souls. For My yoke is easy, and My burden is light" (Matthew 11:28–30).

"Blessed are the meek, for they shall inherit the earth" (Matthew 5:5).

"And behold, I am with you always, to the end of the age" (Matthew 28:20).

"I have said these things to you, that in Me you may have peace. In the world you will have tribulation. But take heart; I have overcome the world" (John 16:33).

"I came that they may have life and have it abundantly" (John 10:10).

All of these promises are true, for they are all from Jesus—the truth.

Satan will continue to lie to you and me and everyone we know. He will fill our lives with as much suffering and difficulty as he can manage. Satan will prowl and roar and ever seek to frighten us and push us away from Jesus. That is true.

But Jesus will continue to tell you and me and everyone we know the truth. He will fill our lives with joy and peace. Jesus will draw near to you and be with you. In the end, He will throw Satan down and cast Satan out, never to bother us again.

Jesus will bring us into the joys of eternal life that are entirely free from Satan and his lies. Jesus will bring us ever deeper into the abundance of His love. Now, today, He invites us to ask, seek, and knock. He invites us to cling to the word of truth. Jesus invites us to bask in Him and all His fullness, for He is full of grace and truth.

Holy Spirit, before Jesus died, He promised us that You would lead us into all truth. As we set down this book and endeavor to live more fully in the light of truth, we pray that You would go before us, with us, and behind us. We pray that You would expose Satan's lies and that You would guide us into all truth, for You live and reign with the Father and the Son, one God, now and forever. Amen.

A final Scripture passage to contemplate:

> Finally, brothers, whatever is true, whatever is honorable, whatever is just, whatever is pure, whatever is lovely, whatever is commendable, if there is any excellence, if there is anything worthy of praise, think about these things. (Philippians 4:8)

COUNTERING SATAN'S LIES

LIE	TRUTH	BIBLE PASSAGE TO REMEMBER
You cannot trust God.	God's Word proves true.	Proverbs 3:4-5
Your value is based on your performance.	Your value is based on Jesus' perfect performance for you.	Hebrews 4:14-16
You need and deserve more.	God knows what you need and will provide it.	Matthew 7:7-11
Life will be better if you seize more control.	All authority in heaven and on earth has been given to Jesus, not to us.	Matthew 5:38–44
You are exempt (from rules, bad news, and good news).	You are a unique member of the Body of Christ.	1 Corinthians 12:27
You should cover up your sins.	Jesus covers your sins by His blood and clothes you with the robe of righteousness.	Romans 4:7
God does not love you.	Jesus loves you, and He always will.	John 15:12
You can and must save yourself.	You have been saved by grace because of Jesus' death and resurrection.	Ephesians 2:8–10
You are alone.	You are not alone. God is always with you.	Matthew 28:20
You are too flawed to be forgiven.	You are forgiven, cleansed, healed, and perfected by Jesus.	Ephesians 1:7

COUNTERING OUR FEARS

FEAR SATAN PREYS ON	GOD'S LOVE THAT CASTS OUT FEAR	BIBLE PASSAGE TO REMEMBER
Being wrong or deceived	Jesus loves you, even when you make mistakes.	John 15:9
Not being admired or valued	God makes you valuable through His own love for you.	1 John 3:1–3
Missing out, enduring scarcity, being deprived	Jesus is your Good Shepherd. You lack nothing.	Psalm 23:1
Being controlled and manipulated by others	God will protect you and be your refuge.	Psalm 18:2
Being without significance or meaning	Your unique significance is a gift of God.	Luke 15:31–32
Being abandoned	God will never abandon you.	Luke 19:10
Being unloved and unwanted	Nothing can separate you from the love of God.	Romans 8:38–39
Being incompetent and helpless	God is your helper.	Hebrews 13:6
Being without security or support	You will dwell securely with Jesus forever.	Psalm 16:9–10
Being too sinful for God to forgive	God removes your sin as far as the east is from the west.	Psalm 103:10–12

ACKNOWLEDGMENTS

Before I began the process of writing a book about Satan, I asked people to pray for me during my normal writing hours. Without them, I imagine this book would have never reached completion. So thank you to Rich Carter, Jim and Betty Marrs, Mark and Anne Heine, and Betty Fraga. And thank you to any and all others who prayed for me as this book became reality.

As I neared the due date for this book, I asked for help and feedback from people I trusted to tell me the truth. So thank you also to Beth Kegley, Caleb Cox, Bethany Ramse, Phil Brandvold, Shelly Schwalm, and my wife, Stephanie. Then the manuscript went on to my editor, Jamie Moldenhauer, whose skill helped the truths of this book become much easier to read.

Throughout this process, my mind returned frequently to classes at Concordia University, St. Paul, with the Rev. Dr. Stephen Stohlmann. Dr. Stohlmann gave language to what I had been experiencing in Satan's attacks. His desire to speak the truth and expose Satan's lies sparked in me a desire to do the same. Though Dr. Stohlmann has transferred to the church triumphant, I hope this book lives up to his standards.